the CUBAN FIVE

Who they are
Why they were framed
Why they should be free

FROM THE PAGES OF THE 'MILITANT'

PATHFINDER
NEW YORK LONDON MONTREAL SYDNEY

Edited by Martín Koppel and Mary-Alice Waters
Copyright © 2013 by Pathfinder Press

ISBN 978-1-60488-043-4
Library of Congress Control Number 2012946872
Manufactured in the United States of America

First edition, 2011
Second edition, 2012
Third edition, 2012
Fourth printing, 2013

Cover design: Tom Tomasko
Cover photo of René González and back cover photo: Bill Hackwell
Back cover photo: Mass rally in Havana demands release of five
Cuban revolutionaries from US prisons, May 1, 2010.

Pathfinder
www.pathfinderpress.com
E-mail: pathfinder@pathfinderpress.com

Contents

* Dates refer to issues of the *Militant* in which articles appeared.

Part II: 'We Will Continue Until Victory'

Part III: Who Are the Cuban Five?

Introductory Note

This new, expanded edition of *The Cuban Five: Who They Are, Why They Were Framed, Why They Should Be Free* is the third to be published in less than a year. That fact alone is a measure of the thirst for more information from those around the world who are learning about Gerardo Hernández, Ramón Labañino, Antonio Guerrero, Fernando González, and René González and want to join the fight for their freedom. In addition to the English- and Spanish-language editions produced simultaneously by Pathfinder Press, work is under way on translations into Farsi and French. We are confident other languages will follow.

Gerardo, Ramón, Antonio, Fernando, and René are five Cubans who were living and working in southern Florida in 1998 when each of them was arrested in coordinated predawn raids by the US government. At that time William Clinton was president.

They were framed up on charges that included conspiracy to commit espionage and, in the case of Gerardo Hernández, conspiracy to commit murder. More than two years later, the five—who proudly acknowledged they were working for the Cuban government—were brought to trial and convicted in federal court in Miami on all counts. The judge imposed maximum sentences. Three were given life without parole.

On September 12, 2012, each of the five will begin serving his fifteenth year in US custody. For Gerardo, Ramón, and Antonio those years have for the most part been hard time in maximum security penitentiaries. Gerardo Hernández, handed two life sentences the court generously allowed him to serve concurrently, and René Gonzalez, now out on parole, faced an additional arbitrary and brutal penalty. Throughout their imprisonment the US government has refused to grant visas to their wives, Adriana Pérez and Olga Salanueva, to enter the United States to visit them.

What were the alleged criminal activities of the Five?

They organized to infiltrate paramilitary and other counterrevolutionary Cuban American groups that have a fifty-year record of planning and carrying out bombings, assassinations, and other assaults on Cubans as well as other supporters of the Cuban Revolution—on the island, in the United States (yes, inside the US), in Puerto Rico, and elsewhere. Their assignment was to keep the Cuban government informed of those deadly operations in order to prevent as many as possible from coming to fruition.

The Cuban Five: Who They Are, Why They Were Framed, Why They Should Be Free tells this story as fully as possible. The articles reprinted here, along with dozens of photos and other graphic displays, are selected from almost 200 news reports and special features on the Cuban Five that have appeared over the last fourteen years in the pages of the *Militant*, a socialist newsweekly published in New York.

The book has three objectives above all.

The first is to explain why "the case of the Cuban Five" is in fact "the case of the Cuban Revolution." Why does the US government so hate and fear the men and women who made the Cuban Revolution and the younger generations who today join them in defending and fighting to advance it? Why are they holding these five—all exemplary products of that revolution—hostage to the Cuban people's refusal to renounce their socialist course and go down on bended knee before Washington?

The second aim is to help working people and youth in the United States recognize the common web of class interests connecting the "justice" meted out by the US cops and courts to the Five with our own life experiences at the hands of that same "justice" system. Especially whenever we resist, whenever we refuse to simply submit to the increasingly brutal exploitation imposed on us by a capitalist system in deepening crisis, whenever we say "enough!" and take up the struggle, whatever the odds.

The United States holds a higher percentage of its population behind bars than any other country on earth. For the US rulers that is not a choice but a necessary precondition for their continued domination at home and abroad. Today Gerardo, Ramón, Antonio, and Fernando find themselves among the 2.3 million men and women in US prisons, and the nearly five million, like René, under some form of probation, parole, or "supervised release." Through no choice of their own, they stand in the front ranks of the class struggle in the United States. And working people in the US who in increasing numbers *are* finding ways to fight back discover in them a worthy example.

The third goal is to provide information that will be a help to all those engaged in this fight worldwide. The new edition for the first time includes not only a presentation of the book made at the Havana International Book Fair in February 2012, but several recent *Militant* articles that continue to deepen our appreciation of the character and revolutionary caliber of each of the Cuban Five— and members of their families.

A number of special features have also been added. These include a political "timeline" of the case of the Five, a summary of charges each was convicted of and sentences each received, and excerpts from opinions by US appeals court justices who reviewed the trial record and would have thrown the convictions out if their rulings had been allowed to stand. Also included is a list of some among the thousands of organizations, institutions, and individuals in the United States and around the world who have voiced support for the fight to win freedom for the Five, as well as statements by some of the most prominent of them.

Credit for these additions goes to individuals and organizations in different parts of the world— from Indonesia and Iran, to France and the United States—who have insistently asked for further information and materials to help them understand and present the case to others who are just now learning about the Cuban Five and coming to support them.

Those requests prompted the preparation of answers in a form designed to be useful to all who are involved in this worldwide effort, including the 350 committees in 114 countries, and the thousands of individuals and hundreds of political organizations, that are working to build what Gerardo Hernández rightly described as the "jury of millions that will make our truth be known."

Mary-Alice Waters
Martín Koppel
SEPTEMBER 1, 2012

NOTE

This third edition of *The Cuban Five* was published prior to the US court ruling that allowed René González to return to Cuba in May 2013. Except for the timeline and the new four-page feature that follows, the articles and other material in this reprint of the book have not been updated.

A NEW STANDARD-BEARER IN THE BATTLE FOR THE FIVE
René González is back in Cuba to stay

RAÚL PUPO/JUVENTUD REBELDE

OMARA GARCÍA MEDEROS/AIN

On May 3, 2013, a new chapter was opened in the international battle to win freedom for the Cuban Five. After serving thirteen years in US prisons, plus half of the additional three-year "supervised release" imposed on him by the US courts, René González announced to the world that he was back in Cuba to stay.

That watershed, which has brought new energy worldwide to the campaign to win the release of Fernando, Antonio, Ramón and Gerardo, is registered in the photos on these pages.

From the Victorville federal penitentiary in California and the Federal Correctional Institute in Marianna, Florida, Gerardo Hernández and Antonio González paid tribute to René in the messages reprinted on the next two pages.

Above: René González addresses convention of Cuba's Federation of University Students, Havana, June 12, 2013. He urged students to "seek out the truth" to "understand why it's necessary for capitalism to disappear as a system." He added, "There are many people you need to reach—you must go outside the classroom. . . . We can't forget there are many youth who are not in school, who produce the wealth with their hands."

Right: René González (center, holding child) and other Havana protesters in front of US Interests Section demand release of remaining members of Cuban Five, September 12, 2013.

ALBERTO BORREGO/GRANMA

'EACH ONE OF THE FIVE IS A LITTLE MORE FREE'

Gerardo Hernández

He could have used the same pretexts as those who quickly decided to plead guilty and cooperate with the authorities. After long years of separation from his wife and older daughter, Olga and Irmita were finally here with him. He'd been able to enjoy the newborn Ivette for barely four months. What to do? Stick to his principles, leave the three of them alone in a foreign country, and once again face years of separation? Or "negotiate" and give them what they asked for in exchange for a pardon and a new life? There was never the slightest doubt in his mind, nor the least hesitation in his conduct.

The prosecutors knew they had very little against him, and they tried to get him out of the way with offers. It bothered them that he sang *El Necio** and they took out their anger on him. No one saw him cry when they separated Olga from

_____

* *El Necio* (The Stubborn Fool) is a 1992 song written by Cuban musician Silvio Rodríguez about remaining steadfast in support of Cuba's socialist revolution in face of the deep economic, social, and political crisis precipitated by the abrupt loss of foreign trade after the collapse of the USSR. It was a defiant response to those, particularly outside the island, who were warning that the revolution was on its last legs and that its supporters should give up the fight and accept a capitalist future in Cuba.

the girls and threw her into a cell. He must have done that in silence, as we all did from outrage and pain when we heard the news, but we never noticed in him the slightest sign of weakening. He served every day of his sentence with dignity, and came out with his head held as high as when he went in, but he would still have to suffer alone the deaths of his brother and his father.

Today we learned that René is in Cuba to stay. Today each one of the Five is a little more free. Part of us is walking through the streets of that island, and we can almost breathe the air and feel the sun burning our skin.

Someone asked me what we will say now that we are not five but four. Mistake! We are five and will continue to be five! If today we must continue the fight, it's not just for the other four, but for René as well, because we know him, and we know he will never be truly free until we're all back in the homeland. The difference now is that this battle, which will be for the Five till the end, now has a new standard-bearer.

Congratulations, René! Your four brothers proudly celebrate with you!

¡Hasta la victoria siempre!

EMILIO HERRERA/PRENSA LATINA

René González in Havana with his wife Olga Salanueva (second from right), their daughters Irma and Ivette (second from left and far right), and Irma's husband, Freeman Acosta, May 6, 2013, after announcing René's definitive return to Cuba.

'WE WERE, ARE, AND WILL BE THE CUBAN FIVE'

Tony Guerrero

That September 12, for which there is no adjective to describe its violence, I was the last to arrive in Miami, and thus, the last to be placed in an extremely cold cell, with a bare mattress, a bedspread, and a roll of toilet paper—all of us in isolation.

The silence was dismal on that 13th floor of the Miami Federal Detention Center. Pure animal instinct makes you walk in circles within that confined space. From time to time, I stopped in front of the narrow pane of glass in the metal door, through which a guard constantly kept an eye on us during his rounds. In a cell facing mine, off to the side, I could see a man who also stopped at his little window from time to time. I saw an austere, bearded face, a bare chest, and asked myself: Who can that guy be? Isn't he cold?

It was René. I didn't know him yet.

During those early days, of which there is still much to be told, they took him and me down to the courtroom. There we were to plead innocent or guilty, which, in our case, was declaring ourselves worthy or unworthy, honest or dishonest, loyal or traitorous. The two of us were certain of our innocence. But there was one, whom I didn't know either, who was going to plead guilty. Each one of us went before the judge separately, but René read betrayal on the face of that character, who was trying to involve me with some story.

Later René told me, "I've got to talk to that guy." I simply asked him to stay calm.

That's how I got to know him.

That's how the five of us became brothers.

For that reason, his freedom is our freedom, and his pain and his joy are also ours.

For that reason, our unjust imprisonment will continue being his imprisonment.

For that reason, we were, are, and will be the Five, merging into one man, one Cuban like millions of compatriots, loyal to their people and to their homeland.

DIONY SANABIA/PRENSA LATINA

Demonstrations on September 12, 2013, fifteenth anniversary of arrest of Cuban Five, demand their release.

Top: In Santo Domingo, Dominican Republic.

Right: In front of White House, Washington, DC.

BILL HACKWELL

WORLDWIDE ACTIONS DEMAND 'FREE THE CUBAN FIVE' ON 15TH ANNIVERSARY OF ARRESTS

EDUARDO RODRÍGUEZ/PRENSA LATINA

Top: In Madrid, Spain, some 200 people protested at US embassy, September 12, 2013. A similar action was held in Barcelona.

Middle: Action in Sydney, Australia, September 14, 2013.

ROBBIE VAN LEEUWEN

Below: Protesters in the island country of Seychelles, in the Indian Ocean, September 30, 2013.

ILONA GERSH/MILITANT

Above: Demonstration in Chicago, September 12, 2013. Herlinda Hernández (left) of Service Employees International Union and another defense campaign supporter, Michael Barry, give out information to passersby.

ALBERTO SALAZAR/PRENSA LATINA

'ONE DAY MY PRISON SHIRT TOO WILL BE HANGING ON A PEG'
Havana Presentation of 'The Cuban Five'

By Mary-Alice Waters

The Cuban Five: Who They Are, Why They Were Framed, Why They Should Be Free was launched at the Havana International Book Fair, February 18, 2012. Speaking at that presentation were Kenia Serrano, president of the Cuban Institute of Friendship with the Peoples (ICAP), which has led the international fight to free the Cuban Five, and Mary-Alice Waters, president of Pathfinder Press and one of the book's editors and authors.

The program included readings in tribute to the Five by two of Cuba's best-known poets, Pablo Armando Fernández and Edel Morales, vice president of the Cuban Book Institute. The event took place in a hall inside the historic La Cabaña fortress overlooking Havana Bay, surrounded by an exhibition of the stunning butterfly paintings of Cuban Five hero Antonio Guerrero, created by him for Havana's Natural History Museum.

In the front rows of the audience were several members of the families of the five revolutionaries—María Eugenia Guerrero, Antonio's sister, and Adriana Pérez, Olga Salanueva, and Rosa Aurora Freijanes, the wives of Gerardo Hernández, René González, and Fernando González respectively. Serrano paid special tribute to the women as "Marianas all," recalling the unshakable steadfastness and courage of Mariana Grajales, one of Cuba's great independence fighters in its nineteenth century struggle against Spanish colonial rule.

Following is the presentation by Mary-Alice Waters.

❧

On behalf of Pathfinder Press, welcome to all, especially to Kenia Serrano, president of the Cuban Institute of Friendship with the Peoples, and to members of the families of Gerardo, Ramón, Antonio, Fernando, and René who are with us.

It's a pleasure to be making the presentation of this book today surrounded by this impressive gallery of Antonio's paintings and accompanied by the music-in-words of Pablo Armando Fernández and Edel Morales.

❧

The Cuban Five is a selection of articles from the pages of the *Militant*, "a socialist newsweekly published in the interests of working people," as its masthead proudly states. With pages both in English and Spanish each week, the *Militant* is circulated and read not only in the United States, Canada, the United Kingdom, Australia, and New Zealand, but elsewhere around the world.

Selected from nearly two hundred *Militant* articles over the years of the fight to free the five combatants, the compilation does not pretend to be

JONATHAN SILBERMAN/MILITANT

Presentation of *The Cuban Five* at Havana International Book Fair, February 2012. From left: Mary-Alice Waters; Kenia Serrano, president of Cuban Institute of Friendship with the Peoples; and poet Edel Morales, vice president of Cuban Book Institute.

a book of record. It doesn't attempt to cover everything of importance about the multifront struggle to win freedom for our comrades. It is published in the hopes it will be used as one of many weapons in that battle. We chose the format because it is easy to produce new editions, adjusting the content as needed by reporting new developments, eliminating items that have been superseded, incorporating new photos and statements of support.

Our pledge is to keep updating the selection—*as long as necessary*. And when it is no longer necessary, we'll republish *The Cuban Five* with a victory introduction!

The book's purpose is to arm those who read it with knowledge about the kind of human beings Gerardo, Ramón, Antonio, Fernando, and René are. The objective is to enable working people the world over, and in the United States especially, to understand what otherwise seems inexplicable:

Why, despite all evidence to the contrary, were our five comrades convicted of conspiracy to engage in espionage against the US government—and, in the case of Gerardo, even conspiracy to commit murder? Why were they locked up in US prisons with sentences up to double life plus fifteen years?

Our aim is to make it possible for those who read the book to connect this nightmare to our own life experiences as working people who refuse to simply surrender our rights, our dignity, the future we are fighting for.

Our goal is to enable a still small but growing vanguard of combative workers—and youth attracted to their struggles—to understand why the fight to win freedom for the Cuban Five is *our* battle, part of the class struggle inside the US as well as internationally.

If there is one thing I hope those here today will take away with you, it is our conviction that the fight for the return of our five Cuban brothers *will be won*, not through the good graces of Barack Obama (or any other president nominated by a party of the imperialist empire), but because of what is changing in the world today—the resistance by working people in the United States and internationally to the consequences *for us* of the deepening capitalist crisis, a crisis still in its opening years. From the streets of Greece and Spain to factories across the US, it is not we who are initiating the fights; it is the employers and their state

apparatus who are forcing those battles upon us.

But more and more—as the people of Cuba have responded many times—working people in the United States are beginning to say, "Enough!" Over the coming months and years of the world capitalist crisis, more will stand and fight. Our very dignity as free human beings is at stake.

"Explaining the otherwise inexplicable" begins with the Cuban Revolution itself. Why did each of the five accept the dangerous mission asked of them—to live and work in the United States, gathering intelligence on Brothers to the Rescue and other counterrevolutionary groups, some of them organized into paramilitary units that function openly in South Florida with Washington's knowledge, if not complicity? Why did each of our compañeros say with pride in the courtroom that if asked to accept that assignment again, they would do so without hesitation?

Their work began years before the Brothers to the Rescue provocations that culminated in the February 1996 shootdown of two of the group's planes in Cuban airspace and led to the murder conspiracy frame-up of Gerardo. That history, however, best exemplifies the pressing necessity of the mission they undertook.

Posturing as a "humanitarian" operation to save Cubans trying to cross the Florida Straits in flimsy crafts, Brothers to the Rescue pilots, led by CIA-trained José Basulto, repeatedly violated Cuban airspace. The group's leaders did so knowing full well that Cuba, like any sovereign country, would defend its people and its territory.

The intent was obvious: to precipitate Cuban military action against intruding civilian planes—flown by US citizens, and taking off from US airstrips—in hopes of provoking military retaliation by Washington. The Cuban government successfully prevented that sequence of events from unfolding, but the Clinton administration was determined to find a way to make the Cuban people pay a heavy price nonetheless. And they did.

It was not only the sharp intensification of the decades-long economic war codified by the Helms-Burton Act. It was the arrest, frame-up, conviction, and draconian sentences meted out to the five outstanding examples of the kind of men and women a genuine socialist revolution made possible.

Without this broader perspective on Washington's goals, working people and youth in the United States have a hard time making sense of why the five are in prison, why humanitarian appeals fall on deaf ears—and why the fight to free them is, above all, a *political* fight in defense of the Cuban Revolution. Only within this historical sweep can they begin to appreciate the caliber of these five revolutionaries and identify with them as the kind of fighters they themselves hope to become.

🙢

Gerardo, Ramón, Antonio, Fernando, and René— like their wives, mothers, and all their loved ones—do not act like victims, much less suffering martyrs nailed to a cross. They act like the proletarian internationalists they are, as revolutionary combatants who take their places on the front lines of battle wherever they find themselves. It's why they are so hated by Washington.

As many of you here well know, there are some 2.3 million men and women incarcerated in the prisons of the United States. It is the country whose prisoners make up a higher percentage of the population than anywhere else on earth. The overwhelming majority are working people framed up and railroaded to jail without trial after being blackmailed by the threat of decades behind bars, and sometimes the death penalty, and pressured into pleading guilty to some "lesser" crime they did not commit. This outrage—*which accounts for 97 percent of all federal "convictions"*—is delicately called "plea bargaining."

It took a decade of bloody civil war followed by a revolutionary struggle in the United States for working people in the nineteenth century to win the Fourteenth Amendment to the US Constitution affirming the right to "equal protection under the law." It will take another revolution in the United States, led by the working class and its allies, to make that constitutional right a reality for working people.

Within the working class, and among African Americans and other oppressed peoples especially, there is hardly a family that doesn't have some relative who is or has been in jail, or that doesn't know someone among friends, acquaintances, and fellow workers who is serving or has served time, or is now on probation or parole and being carefully watched.

Frame-ups against workers have always been an integral part of the system of class rule. What was done to the Cuban Five is something all too familiar to the vast majority of working people in the United States. It is one reason, as they learn the facts, that workers identify with Gerardo, Ramón, Antonio, Fernando, and René and respect them.

We know firsthand the kind of political work

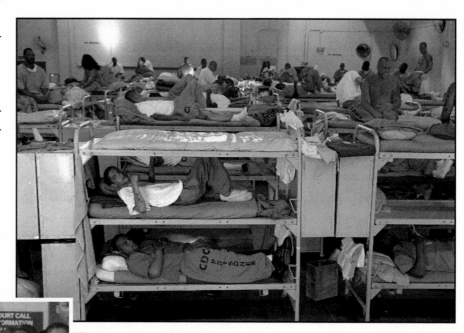

"There are some 2.3 million in US prisons, the large majority of them working people, most railroaded to jail without trial after being pressured into pleading guilty to some 'lesser' crime they did not commit," said Waters. **Above:** California State Prison in Los Angeles, August 2006. **Left:** Vincent Thames (center) and Terrill Swift (right) leave Chicago court, November 2011, after judge ordered new trial for rape and murder they and two others "confessed" to under police coercion. The four spent more than 15 years behind bars.

carried out by each of the five while in prison. We know it not only from what they themselves describe in letters, but from the not infrequent requests for subscriptions to the *Militant* and copies of Pathfinder books from prisoners with whom one or another of the compañeros has crossed paths. Both the *Militant* and Pathfinder have long had special reduced prices for prisoners.

One such recent request was from a prisoner asking for a copy of *Che Guevara Talks to Young People,* saying he had seen a copy of *The Cuban Five* and was impressed because he knew one of them, Antonio. "He and I have discussed different subjects about the world we all share," the prisoner wrote. "Your help in their struggle is appreciated by me as well as by people all over the world."

❧

Why are we confident that together we will win the battle for the freedom of our five comrades?

The capitalist economic crisis that exploded with such violence in 2008 is having far-reaching consequences for the working class in the United States. The impact of high levels of long-term unemployment, the millions of families who have lost their homes, medical care, pensions, savings, and hopes for the future—the impact of all this continues to be devastating.

For millions of workers who eventually find employment again, it is usually at wages that are a fraction of what they earned before. Others, also numbering in the growing millions, have simply stopped looking for a job and are no longer counted as part of the labor force. They aren't even included in the government's most widely used monthly unemployment figures.

The brutal speedup, longer hours, and intensification of labor, along with the slashing of wages, especially for new hires, have given employers a taste of blood. In factory after factory, owners are demanding new concessions on wages and working conditions and then locking out workers who refuse to accept the new "contract" terms.

This doesn't reflect a *choice* by the US capitalists. It's the course along which they *must* press if they are to recover from the crisis their system—not the workers—produced. Lower wage levels; two or more "tiers" of workers doing the very same jobs alongside each other with sharply different pay and conditions; a growing reserve army of unemployed workers; trade unions that can no longer defend their own contracts, much less act as tribunes of the oppressed and exploited; rising homelessness; large-scale incarceration of angry young workers—especially African American: all these are *necessary preconditions* for capitalist recovery.

You have heard a lot about the activities that have taken place under the name of "Occupy Wall Street" or "Occupy" whatever else. Unless you are a reader of the *Militant,* however, you are probably unaware of the breadth of labor resistance in the United States.

The Cuban Five is not the

SCHOMBURG CENTER/NEW YORK PUBLIC LIBRARY

"It took a bloody civil war and revolutionary struggle in the US for working people to win the 14th amendment to the US Constitution affirming the right to 'equal protection under the law.' It will take another revolution, led by the working class and its allies, to make that constitutional right a reality," said Waters. **Above:** After US Civil War, recently enfranchised Blacks in Lincoln County, Georgia, rifles in hand, ford a creek on their way to vote.

only thing the bourgeois media refuses to cover. But the silence is not a conspiracy. They don't have to conspire. No one has to tell them it is not in their interests for workers to be able to learn from the example of others who are resisting the conditions imposed upon them.

Yet what is happening in the course of these labor battles will have far more lasting consequences than the discontent registered by the Occupy phenomenon. Above all, it is important because vanguard workers are learning of each other and extending the hand of solidarity to each other across industries, regions, and national borders.

From sugar workers not far from the Canadian border in northern Minnesota and North Dakota, to tire workers in Ohio, to workers protesting anti-immigrant laws in Alabama, to longshoremen in the state of Washington on the West Coast, the labor battles have an intensity and sharpness that has not been seen in the United States for some time.*

In the last weeks alone, during a confrontation with the port workers in Longview, Washington,

DAWN DES BRISAY

"As they go through their own battles, workers learn firsthand how the cops and courts are stacked against those who refuse to accept the conditions capitalism imposes on us. And above all, how the cops and courts are used against those they cannot break," said Waters. "These militants come to admire the five Cuban combatants and will come to emulate their determination and courage." **Above:** Port of Longview, Washington State, September 2011. Cops assault dock workers at protest against bosses' efforts to drive union out of grain terminal.

---

* Some 1,300 members of the Bakery, Confectionery, Tobacco Workers and Grain Millers Union in the Upper Midwest have been fighting a lockout by American Crystal Sugar since August 1, 2011, after they refused bosses' concession contract demands.

Some 1,050 members of United Steelworkers Local 207L were locked out November 28, 2011, in Findlay, Ohio, after rejecting Cooper Tire and Rubber Co.'s contract demands to cut wages, speed up work, and establish lower pay and benefits for new hires. The lockout ended after workers voted to accept a contract offer February 27, 2012.

Members of International Longshore and Warehouse Union (ILWU) Local 21 led a fight against attempt by EGT Development to shut the union out of its terminal in the Port of Longview, Washington. If successful, EGT would have set a precedent with the first West Coast grain terminal run without ILWU labor in eight decades. After an eight-month struggle, EGT conceded to hiring ILWU labor.

the Obama administration ordered the Coast Guard to escort an incoming ship and protect it as it was being loaded by scab labor. At the last minute, a more serious confrontation was averted when a settlement restoring union protection for longshoremen at a major company on those docks was won.

More than 200 port workers were arrested in the course of this standoff, however, and charged with various felonies for which some of them still face costly court battles and the possibility of lengthy prison sentences if convicted.

These are the kinds of battlefronts where *The Cuban Five* is sold, and where dozens of workers with subscriptions to the *Militant*—the paper in which these articles were originally printed—are not only reading about themselves and each others' battles. They are reading about Gerardo, Ramón, Antonio, Fernando, and René week after week. As they go through their own experiences, they rapidly learn firsthand how the cops and courts are stacked against those who fight, who resist, who refuse to accept the conditions capitalism imposes on us. And above all, how the cops and courts are used against those they cannot break. These militants begin to understand and admire the five Cuban combatants and in the course of the battles before us will come to emulate their determination and courage.

At the time the West Coast longshore battle was intensifying, a showing of Antonio's prison paintings—like those that surround us here—was organized by the teachers union and students at one of the colleges in nearby Seattle.

One of the port workers, a woman who had been arrested during an action organized by the union and was facing trumped-up felony charges, saw a postcard for the Seattle art showing, a card that reproduced Antonio's painting of his prison shirt. Her response—with a touch of apprehension masked by determination and pride—was, "One day my prison shirt too will be hanging on a peg."

From the longshore workers to the sugar workers and beyond, these are the men and women who in growing numbers will belong to what Gerardo has accurately referred to as the "jury of millions" that will liberate them. It is along this road, where class battles are intensifying because of the workings of the capitalist system itself, that their freedom will be won.

That is what gives confidence to those like us inside the United States who are fighting to win the freedom of the Five.

It is why the publication of *The Cuban Five*, and how it will be used around the world, is so important.

MARCH 12, 2012

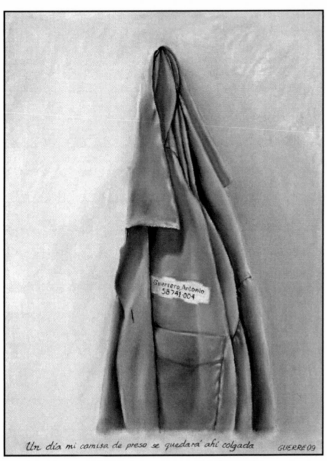

One day my prison shirt will be left hanging there, pastel by Antonio Guerrero.

TIMELINE IN CASE OF CUBAN FIVE

January 1, 1959: US-backed Batista dictatorship falls as popular insurrection sweeps country, spearheaded by Rebel Army victories and July 26 Movement leadership under Fidel Castro. Cuban workers and peasants begin transforming Cuban society and its economic foundations in their interests, as the revolutionary government itself is transformed.

January 1959–today: Washington from outset organizes to reverse momentum of popular mobilizations and to overthrow new government. Among its main instruments are armed counterrevolutionary Cuban groups organized and financed by large property owners and former Batista henchmen seeking to restore lost prerogatives. Centered in South Florida, these groups, increasingly trained and organized by CIA, operate with impunity on US soil. Over five decades, nearly 3,500 Cubans are killed and 2,100 injured in attacks, most originating in US.

1975–91: Acting on Cuban Revolution's decades of anti-imperialist internationalism, more than 375,000 Cubans, including best of post-1959 generations, volunteer for combat in Angola, helping newly independent government defeat invasions by South Africa's white supremacist regime. Among volunteers are René González (1977–79), Fernando González (1987–89), and Gerardo Hernández (1989–90).

1989–91: Disintegration of Soviet-bloc regimes leads to abrupt collapse of 85 percent of Cuba's foreign trade, precipitating severe economic crisis Cubans refer to as the Special Period. US government policies encourage large numbers of Cubans hit by extreme hardship to cross Florida Straits to US on dangerously flimsy rafts and boats. US-based counterrevolutionary groups, convinced revolutionary government in Havana is about to fall, step up operations.

December 1990 on: René González (1990), Ramón Labañino (1992), Antonio Guerrero (1992), Gerardo Hernández (1994), and Fernando González (1997) begin intelligence-gathering missions in South Florida to inform Cuban authorities of provocations and violent attacks planned by counterrevolutionary Cuban American groups on Cubans and supporters of the Cuban Revolution in Cuba, the US, and elsewhere.

May 1991: CIA-trained José Basulto launches Brothers to the Rescue (BTTR) in Miami, depicting it as "humanitarian" effort to rescue "rafters."

Mid-1994–February 1996: US-Cuba migration accords lead to drop in numbers trying to cross straits. Brothers to the Rescue steps up flights penetrating Cuban airspace. The aim is to provoke Cuban military action against unarmed US civilian planes piloted by US citizens, in order to precipitate military retaliation by Washington. Havana repeatedly warns BTTR and Washington that Cuba will defend its territory and airspace against continued intrusions.

February 24, 1996: In the twenty-sixth incursion in 20 months, three Brothers to the Rescue planes again fly into Cuba's airspace and refuse to heed warnings to turn back. Two are shot down by Cuban air force. Four pilots die. Three are US citizens, one a permanent resident. Basulto's plane gets away. BTTR provocations over Cuban airspace cease.

March 12, 1996: In retaliation, President Clinton signs Helms-Burton Act sharply escalating decades-long US economic war against Cuba.

1995–98: FBI agents conduct undercover surveillance of Hernández, Labañino, Guerrero, Fernando González, René González, and others. Beginning August 1996, with warrants issued by the Foreign Intelligence Surveillance Court, which operates behind closed doors inside Justice Department, FBI starts secretly breaking into their South Florida apartments and copying computer files.

April–November 1997: String of bombings of Havana hotels and tourist sites organized by US-based groups. Italian-Canadian visitor Fabio Di Celmo is killed in blast at Hotel Copacabana.

June 16–17, 1998: At Cuba's initiative, FBI and Cuban State Security officials meet in Havana. FBI is given voluminous evidence collected by Cuban intelligence on plans for assassinations, bombings, and other attacks on Cubans and supporters of the revolution in Cuba and elsewhere by US-based groups.

September 12, 1998: In predawn weekend raids, FBI agents arrest 10 people they accuse of being part of "Cuban spy ring." Four others for whom arrest warrants were issued are never found. Five of those taken into custody "cooperate" with prosecution, while Washington begins building frame-up of Hernández, Labañino, Guerrero, Fernando González, and René González, whom US officials are unable to break.

October 2, 1998: Federal grand jury hands down indictments. Charges range from acting as an unregistered foreign agent to conspiracy to commit espionage.

September 1998–February 2000: Denied bail, the five revolutionaries are held for 17 months in Special Housing Unit (SHU) punishment cells—the "hole"—at Miami's Federal Detention Center. Each is initially subjected to months of solitary confinement—Hernández and Labañino the longest, six months.

May 7, 1999: Federal prosecutors charge Hernández with conspiracy to commit murder for alleged role in 1998 shootdown of Brothers to the Rescue planes.

November 1999–June 2000: Six-year-old Elián González, Cuban boy whose mother died at sea, is picked up by US Coast Guard and turned over to distant relatives in Miami. Despite mounting worldwide condemnation, Clinton administration for six months refuses to return him to his father in Havana. In April 2000, immigration police commandos raid home and seize the child, who returns to Cuba with father in June. Throughout confrontation, Cuban American rightists stage street actions demanding child be kept in US.

January 5, 2000: Defense attorneys for Cuban Five file first of multiple motions requesting change of venue on basis that they cannot receive impartial trial in Miami. Each is denied by federal district judge Joan Lenard.

August 16, 2000: Immigration cops arrest Olga Salanueva in what is a failed effort to pressure husband René González to testify against other four. Charged with violating conditions of residency, after three months in state prison Salanueva is deported to Cuba, days before trial begins.

November 27, 2000: Frame-up trial opens in US federal district court in Miami, with Judge Lenard presiding. During one of longest trials in US history, three retired US generals and a retired admiral testify no evidence of espionage exists. In closing days, prosecution informs court it faces "insurmountable hurdle" in proving Hernández *intended* shootdown of Brothers to the Rescue planes to occur over international waters, a burden of proof central to the conspiracy to commit murder charge brought against Hernández.

June 8, 2001: Each of five is convicted on all counts against him.

June 17, 2001: The five issue a "Message to the American People," saying they are "in no way repentant of what we have done to defend our country. We declare ourselves not guilty and simply take comfort in the fact that we have honored our duty to our people and our homeland."

June 26, 2001: The five are stripped of all personal belongings and returned to "the hole" for 48 days.

September 11, 2001: Attacks on World Trade Center and Pentagon. In name of "war against terrorism," US government subsequently enacts USA Patriot Act and implements other measures curtailing constitutional rights.

October 7, 2001: US government launches Afghanistan war.

December 12–27, 2001: Cuban Five are sentenced—Hernández is given two life terms plus 15 years; Labañino, life plus 18 years; Guerrero, life plus 10 years; Fernando González, 19 years; René

González, 15 years. Each is moved to a different federal prison across US.

April 2002: Salanueva's first visa request to visit René is denied. Since then, Washington has denied every visa application and declared her "permanently ineligible" to enter US.

July 25, 2002: With visa issued by Washington, Adriana Pérez travels to the US to visit husband Gerardo Hernández. At Houston airport FBI detains her for 11 hours. They interrogate her, then deport her to Cuba. US government has subsequently denied every visa application.

February 28–March 4, 2003: On eve of war against Iraq, each of Five is thrown into solitary confinement. US officials announce it is for "national security" reasons and they may be kept in hole for a year or longer.

March 19, 2003: US government launches invasion and occupation of Iraq.

March 18–April 8, 2003: Cuban government rolls up network of 75 "dissidents" involved in activities financed by US government programs and run by US diplomatic personnel in Havana. Tried and convicted of working with US government officials and agencies to undermine Cuban government, they receive sentences ranging from 6 to 28 years.

March 31, 2003: The Five are released from solitary confinement.

April–May 2003: Despite disruption of preparations because of restricted access to the Five during month of solitary confinement, defense team files first appeals before 11th Circuit Court in Atlanta.

May 27, 2005: UN Working Group on Arbitrary Detentions issues report concluding that prosecution of Cuban Five did not meet "the standards of a fair trial" and their imprisonment was of "an arbitrary character."

August 9, 2005: Three-judge US appeals court panel in Atlanta unanimously overturns convictions and orders new trial, citing "a perfect storm" of bias created by negative pretrial publicity in Miami-Dade County.

October 31, 2005: Appeals court agrees to US government demand to set aside ruling by 3-judge panel and conduct review by full court.

August 9, 2006: In 10–2 decision, appeals court restores convictions, ruling that Miami trial venue was adequate. Other appeal issues are remanded to 3-judge panel.

September 2006: *Miami Herald* reports that well-known Miami reporters, whose articles helped fuel bias against Cuban Five during trial, received payments from US government's Office of Cuba Broadcasting at that time. Subsequently, Freedom of Information Act requests and further research by supporters of the five establish that $370,000 was paid to seven reporters since 1999, $80,000 of that to five reporters during trial. This information, unknown at time of trial, is basis for habeas corpus appeals by defense.

June 4, 2008: Appeals panel in 2–1 ruling upholds convictions but vacates sentences of Labañino, Guerrero, and Fernando González as excessive. Judges acknowledge "no top secret information was gathered or transmitted" by Labañino, Guerrero, or Hernández and life sentences were thus inconsistent with federal guidelines. Court rejects vacating Hernández's life sentence on espionage conspiracy charge, saying that second life sentence he is serving concurrently renders it moot.

January 30, 2009: Lawyers for Cuban Five appeal to Supreme Court. Twelve "friend of the court" briefs are subsequently filed on behalf of Five, while Justice Department asks court not to hear case.

June 15, 2009: Supreme Court declines to review appeal.

October 13, 2009: Guerrero is resentenced by judge Lenard, reducing life term to 21 years and 10 months.

December 3, 2009: Cuban government arrests Alan Gross, contractor for US State Department's Agency for International Development, during his fifth visit to Cuba that year. He is held on evidence of distributing sophisticated satellite communication equipment to selected individuals as part of US covert operation against Cuba. Washington claims Gross was in Cuba as private citizen helping Jewish community establish contact with Jewish groups elsewhere in the world.

December 8, 2009: Labañino's sentence is reduced from life to 30 years, and Fernando González's from 19 years to 17 years and nine months.

June 10, 2010: With direct appeals exhausted, defense

attorneys file habeas corpus motion on behalf of Hernández. Over subsequent months, similar motions are filed for Labañino, Guerrero, and Fernando González.

July 7, 2010: Cuban government announces release within four months of the 58 remaining "dissidents" convicted in 2003 for actions financed and directed by US government personnel in Cuba.

August 2010: Judith Gross is given visa by Cuban government to visit her jailed husband, Alan Gross. The couple are given a house for themselves alone at Tarará beach, near Havana, for a weekend.

November 2010: As part of a "confidential diplomatic accommodation" between US and Cuban governments that is not disclosed at the time, Salanueva is allowed to enter US and briefly see husband one time "in exchange for a family visit of an American prisoner being held in Cuba." In stark contrast to consideration shown Judith and Alan Gross by Cuban government, she is separated from her children and confined to a hotel under armed guard throughout stay.

February 16, 2011: Attorneys for René González file motion requesting he be allowed to serve his upcoming parole in Cuba.

March 12, 2011: Gross is convicted by Cuban court and given 15 years in prison for "acts against the territorial independence or integrity of the state."

September 7-14, 2011: Former New Mexico governor Bill Richardson travels to Havana with White House offer to waive probation for René González in exchange for Cuba's release of Alan Gross, whom Richardson publicly describes as a "hostage." Cuban government rejects proposal, saying solution of Gross case must be "from a humanitarian point of view and on the basis of reciprocity."

September 16, 2011: Judge Lenard denies motion requesting René González's return to Cuba.

October 7, 2011: After 13 years and 24 days in prison, René González begins three years of "supervised release" in US.

December 24, 2011: Cuban government announces release of 2,900 individuals serving prison terms for nonviolent crimes, including all those labeled "prisoners of conscience" by various international anti–Cuban Revolution "human rights" organizations.

March 30, 2012: By court agreement, René González travels to Cuba for two weeks to visit terminally ill brother Roberto, who dies in June.

June 6, 2012: Attorneys for Hernández file motion asking for discovery on US government payments to members of Miami media during trial.

September 12, 2012: Hernández, Labañino, Guerrero, Fernando González, and René González begin fifteenth year in US custody.

April 22, 2013: René González returns to Cuba under two-week release by federal court to attend memorial for his father, who died earlier in the month.

May 3, 2013: Judge Lenard rules that René González can serve the remaining year and a half of his supervised release in Cuba on condition he renounce his US citizenship. Three days later González signs papers and confirms he is in Cuba to stay.

PART I

*Why and How Washington
Framed the Cuban Five*

Around the world: Support for the fight to free the Cuban Five

Right: Protest in front of US embassy in La Paz, Bolivia, September 12, 2007. Sign reads, "Freedom for the 5 prisoners of the empire."

Middle right: March in Beirut organized by Lebanese Committee of Solidarity for Release of the Five Cuban Heroes, September 2011.

Below: Picket in Stockholm, Sweden, September 12, 2009.

CATHARINA TIRSEN/MILITANT

PAUL PEDERSON/MILITANT

Above: Members of African National Congress Women's League and FOCUS, a Cuban solidarity network, march to US embassy in Pretoria, South Africa, December 10, 2010.

HOW THE FRAME-UP BEGAN

By Martín Koppel

In the early morning hours of Saturday, September 12, 1998, FBI agents raided homes across Miami and the surrounding area. They arrested ten people, ransacking their apartments and seizing personal belongings. With much fanfare, officials of the Clinton administration's Justice and State Departments announced they had discovered a "Cuban spy network" in South Florida.

The big business media reported that those arrested were accused of trying to "penetrate" the Pentagon's Southern Command, based in Miami, as well as to pass US military secrets to the Cuban government, "infiltrate anti-Castro groups," and "manipulate U.S. media and political organizations."

They had sought "to strike at the very heart of our national security system and our very democratic process," US Attorney Thomas Scott alleged at a highly publicized press conference at FBI headquarters in North Miami Beach.

Federal prosecutors singled out five of those arrested as their main targets: Gerardo Hernández, Ramón Labañino, Antonio Guerrero, Fernando González, and René González. The government said they faced espionage charges carrying sentences of up to life in prison.

The truth is that the Cuban Five, as their case has become known internationally, were framed up by the US government.

What was the "spy" activity in which they were allegedly engaged?

The five Cubans explained—publicly and proudly—that they had accepted assignments to keep the government of Cuba informed about counterrevolutionary groups based in South Florida that have a long record of carrying out murderous attacks on Cuba from US soil. Just the previous year, in 1997, there had been a string of bombings of hotels in Havana in which an Italian Canadian visitor was killed.

Not only has Washington done nothing to prevent such attacks—it has given these groups a green light throughout more than five decades of US diplomatic, economic, and military aggression against the Cuban Revolution.

In 2001 the five were convicted after a trial marked by numerous violations of rights guaranteed by the first ten amendments to the US Constitution. They were found guilty despite the fact that federal prosecutors admitted that none of the five had ever handled a single piece of paper classified by the US government.

Hernández was sentenced to two life terms, Labañino and Guerrero to life in prison, René González to fifteen years, and Fernando González to nineteen years.

Purpose of frame-up

The railroading of the Cuban Five had a double purpose.

It was one more attempt by Washington to punish the workers and farmers of revolutionary Cuba for having the audacity to make a socialist revolution ninety miles from US shores and set an example for working people worldwide fighting against exploitation and oppression.

The frame-up was also aimed against workers and farmers here in the United States. The message was clear: think twice before standing up to the employers and their government—this is how we treat those determined to fight.

But the US ruling class underestimated the resistance by these five Cuban revolutionaries. And the rulers misjudged how the treatment the Cubans have been subjected to would be seen by increasing numbers of people.

The Cuban Five, in fact, have been on the front lines of those fighting against assaults by the employers and their government on the rights and living conditions of working people in the United States and worldwide. Not only have they stood up to harsh treatment by their jailers, including months in solitary confinement, as well as the restriction or outright denial of visas for their loved ones to visit them. They have also reached out in solidarity to many—both inside and outside prison walls, in the US and abroad—who refuse to accept the brutalities of capitalist "justice."

This record is consistent with the example they set and the responsibilities they shouldered in Cuba, whether as student leaders or as internationalist combatants among the hundreds of thousands of Cuban volunteers who helped defeat the racist government of South Africa when it invaded the newly independent country of Angola.

Over the years, the frame-up, denial of constitutional protections, and arbitrary treatment of the Cuban Five by US authorities have led growing numbers to demand their release. They have become an example to others resisting exploitation and oppression, from meat packers jailed and deported for working without proper papers, to those opposing the execution in 2011 of Troy Davis, a Black man in Georgia framed up by police.

The five are well aware that their battle for freedom is a long-term one. Because of their refusal to give up, the frame-up has suffered some cracks.

In 2005 a federal appeals court panel overturned their convictions on the basis that they had been "unable to obtain a fair and impartial trial" due to "pretrial publicity surrounding the case." A year later, after the US government challenged that ruling, the full appeals court restored the convictions.

Then in 2008 a third appeals court decision, while upholding the convictions, threw out the sentences against three of the five—including two life sentences—as being excessive even by US sentencing standards. Those terms were reduced in late 2009.[1]

_____

1. See Part II, "Sentence Reduced for Antonio Guerrero" and "Fernando González and Ramón Labañino Win Reduced Sentences."

That the five have been locked up since 1998 leads many people, as they learn the facts, to say: Enough is enough. Free them now!

Refuse to 'cooperate' with government

In September 1998, a few days after their arrests, Hernández, Labañino, Guerrero, René González, and Fernando González were dragged before Federal Magistrate Barry Garber, who ordered them held without bail at Miami's Federal Detention Center. "Each represents a danger to the community," Garber stated, agreeing with the prosecutors. They were assigned court-appointed attorneys.

"The goal now for prosecutors is to persuade the alleged agents to cooperate," the _Miami Herald_ reported September 16, citing unnamed government sources.

Ramón Labañino described what happened to him: "Everything started on Sept. 12, 1998, at about 5:30 a.m. at home, when we were detained and taken to FBI headquarters in Miami for a 'persuasive' interview, where they asked us to collaborate and betray our country with promises offered in return. Obviously I had nothing to say, and after they were sure they were getting nowhere, they put us in a car and took us to the Federal Detention Center in downtown Miami, where we've been all this time."

Labañino wrote these lines to his wife, Elizabeth Palmeiro, in January 2001, as his trial was under way.

Under pressure, five of the ten detainees soon pleaded guilty on lesser charges—acting as an unregistered agent of a foreign government—and agreed to testify against the others. Among them were two married couples with children who were threatened with long prison terms and loss of parental authority over their children. In early 2000 those who bowed to US government pressure to "cooperate" were sentenced to jail terms of between three and a half and seven years, with promises of early release and federal witness protection.

Meanwhile, the Cuban Five were kept isolated in punishment cells for seventeen months, from September 1998 until early February 2000, the first six months of which were solitary confinement—no visitors and no contact even with other prisoners including each other. Locked in "the hole" twenty-three hours a day, each of them was given only an hour of "recreation" to stretch their legs outside cramped, damp, moldy cells.

A federal grand jury brought a thirty-three-count indictment. The five pleaded not guilty to all the charges, which included the following:

• Each was accused of "acting as an agent of the Republic of Cuba without registering with the Attorney General," and of "conspiring" to do so.

• Guerrero, Hernández, and Labañino were charged with "conspiracy to gather and transmit national defense information," a charge frequently shortened in court documents to "conspiracy to commit espionage."

• Hernández was charged with "conspiracy to commit murder."

• Each was accused of various lesser charges such as possession of false identification documents.

• And at the sentencing hearing *after* the trial was over, Federal Judge Joan Lenard augmented the charges against Labañino and Fernando González by claiming they were guilty of "obstruction of justice" for using false names when first arraigned. On that basis, the two were given "enhanced" (cop-speak for "longer") sentences.[2]

The initial indictment was brought in early October 1998. But the charge against Hernández of "conspiracy to commit murder" was added in May 1999, after it became clear to the government that it had failed to break the defendants' spirits despite months of solitary confinement.

In an unprecedented legal move, US officials charged Hernández with responsibility for an action by a sovereign government—Cuba's 1996 shootdown of two planes flown over its territory by Brothers to the Rescue, a right-wing outfit that had repeatedly violated Cuban airspace despite multiple, widely publicized warnings.

2. On December 6, 2011, government prosecutors petitioned Judge Lenard to maintain the frame-up convictions and "enhanced" sentences of Fernando González and Ramón Labañino. The prosecutors were responding to motions the two filed in August and September 2011 to obtain hearings for the presentation of new evidence.

Olga Salanueva (left) and Irma Sehwerert, wife and mother of René González, speak in Havana, December 11, 2007. FBI and US immigration cops arrested Salanueva, then deported her on November 21, 2000, six days before the opening of the trial of René and the other four Cuban revolutionaries. Since then, Washington has repeatedly denied Salanueva entry to see her husband, and in 2008 informed her she was "permanently ineligible" for a visa.

Cops jail, deport Olga Salanueva

Federal officials tried other ways to break the five Cubans, but failed. One particularly crude method was their arrest and deportation of Olga Salanueva as a club against her husband, René González.

Salanueva wrote an account of what happened in *Letters of Love and Hope: The Story of the Cuban Five*, a collection of correspondence between the Cuban Five and their families. González, who was born in the United States and grew up in Cuba, moved to Florida in 1990. Salanueva joined him six years later, becoming a US permanent resident. They have two daughters, Irma, born in Cuba, and Ivette, born in the United States.

On August 16, 2000, almost two years after the arrest of her husband, FBI and Immigration and Naturalization Service cops arrested Salanueva. They confiscated her green card. "They told me that I knew about my husband's activities and that, as a result, my residency was invalid," she wrote. "I was taken to the state prison in Fort Lauderdale."

"The real objective of my detention," she explained, "was to pressure René into signing a confession prepared by the Southern Florida District Attorney in which he would declare himself guilty and testify against the other defendants." Federal officials warned him that Salanueva, as a permanent resident, could also be charged. González refused to sign the confession and she was arrested three days later.

On the way to jail, the cops took Salanueva, dressed in an orange prison jumpsuit, to see González at the Federal Detention Center. "They wanted to show him that they had made good on their threat and that our daughters and I were at their mercy. He looked at me and said, 'You look good in orange!' Even in front of the guards, he hadn't lost his sense of humor." That was the last time she saw him.

"I didn't cry that day," Salanueva added. "When you're among friends you cry—but not in front of your enemies. Dignity gives you strength and steels you."

During the three months Salanueva was jailed, González was not given her letters. "It was clearly an effort to try to unbalance him emotionally, since he did not know anything about me directly and the beginning of the trial was near," she noted.

They were barred from speaking to each other by phone. In a gesture of solidarity, a Peruvian-born coworker at Salanueva's telemarketing job helped them get around that obstacle. "I called her and she recorded my message for René," Salanueva explained. "He did the same. He called her, listened to my recording and then recorded" a message for Olga.

On November 21, 2000, six days before the trial of the five began, Olga Salanueva was deported to Cuba. Since then the US government has repeatedly denied her a visa to see her husband. She, along with other relatives of the men, has never stopped fighting for the release of the Five.

JULY 7, 2008

PART OF A WIDER ASSAULT ON RIGHTS OF WORKING PEOPLE

By Martín Koppel

The railroading of the Cuban Five is part of a broader assault by the capitalist rulers and their government on the rights and living standards of working people. That assault has escalated over the past decade and a half. It has done so under both Democratic and Republican administrations, as the capitalists' long-term crisis of production forces them to intensify exploitation and generates increasing working-class resistance.

From their arrests in 1998 to the trial and imprisonment of the five men—two who are US citizens because they were born here, and three Cuban-born immigrants—every aspect of this case has been a lesson in the workings of capitalist "justice." The story of the Cuban Five is also an education: either the first ten amendments to the US Constitution must be defended in struggle by working people, or the rights they guarantee will be taken from us. The class struggle is not static. There is no neutral ground.

The US government has used the case to weaken protections against "unreasonable searches and seizures" guaranteed by the Fourth Amendment to the Constitution. FBI agents acknowledged that for three years starting in 1995, they spied on and repeatedly broke into the south Florida homes of all five men. Under the cover of a federal warrant, they conducted electronic spying on their apartments, secretly recorded their phone conversations, copied computer files, and seized family photos, personal correspondence, and other belongings, government officials told the press.

"FBI agents ransacked the $850-a-month, one-bedroom apartment" of Gerardo Hernández, Reuters news agency reported September 16, 1998. "They took everything," Henry Raisman, his building manager said.

"They have three years of wiretaps, room bugs, even surreptitious entries—burglaries—and they don't have any specifics," said Jack Blumenfeld, an attorney for Antonio Guerrero, according to the October 6, 1998, *Miami Herald*. He spoke at the time a federal grand jury brought indictments against the five.

Blumenfeld noted that the FBI conducted these break-ins despite the fact that the indictments did not allege a single act of espionage against the US government. None of the 1,400 pages presented as evidence at the trial showed that the defendants had handled any classified information.

How did the US Justice Department get around the fact that they could prove no acts of espionage? By bringing charges of "conspiracy."

"Conspiracy has always been the charge used by the prosecution in political cases," defense attorney Leonard Weinglass explained in an interview quoted by the National Lawyers Guild in June 2008. Such a charge frees the government from having to prove an illegal action, only a vague "agreement" to commit such an action at some unspecified future time.[1]

The trial jury "was asked to find that there was an agreement to commit espionage. The government never had to prove that espionage actually happened. It could not have proven that espionage occurred," Weinglass noted.

---

1. Just in the past seventy-five years, the US rulers have used "conspiracy" charges time and again to target trade unionists, fighters for Black rights, Puerto Rican and Mexican-American fighters, and communists. In 1941 conspiracy laws were used to frame up, convict, and railroad to prison eighteen leaders of the Minnesota truck drivers union and Socialist Workers Party for organizing opposition to Washington's entry into the imperialist slaughter of World War II. In 1953 they were used to convict and execute Ethel and Julius Rosenberg for conspiracy to commit espionage during time of war by allegedly passing information about the atomic bomb to the Soviet government.

Numerous other constitutional protections were undermined by actions of the US government during the trial against the five. This included the use of evidence that, on grounds of "national security," the defendants and their attorneys were denied the same access to as prosecutors (accounting for more than 80 percent of the documentary evidence introduced by the government). The judge also rejected defense motions to move the proceedings out of Miami, despite the "pervasive community sentiment and extensive publicity both before and during the trial," as cited by one of the two dissenting judges in the 2006 appellate court review.

Before the trial: 17 months in the 'hole'

For thirty-three months, from their arrests through the end of the trial, the five were held without bail at the Federal Detention Center in Miami. They were kept in isolation cells—the notorious "hole"—for seventeen months before the trial, the first several months of which were solitary confinement. They were eventually allowed contact with each other only due to the repeated efforts of their attorneys and Washington's realization that such treatment could not break any of them.[2]

After each of the five was convicted on the frame-up charges, and before the sentencing, they were returned to punishment cells for another forty-eight days while the judge went on vacation. This vindictive move came after the five issued a "Message to the American People," published in the Cuban press, reaffirming that they were not guilty of the charges against them and declaring that they were "in no way repentant of what we have done to defend our country."

And in March 2003, on the eve of the US invasion of Iraq, the men, by then locked up in five prisons across the country, were placed in solitary once again—this time, under even more restrictive conditions known as the "box"—a hole within the "hole." They were denied communication with their attorneys by telephone or letter, and all their writing materials were confiscated. The Justice Department said only that this action was for unspecified "national security" reasons and could last as long as a year.[3]

Weinglass, who gained admission to visit Hernández once during that time, wrote: "He is confined in a very small cell barely three paces wide, with no windows and only a slot in the metal door through which food is passed. His clothes were taken from him and he is allowed to wear only underpants and a T-shirt, but no shoes. He cannot tell if it is day or night. His is the only cell [in the prison] where the lights are on twenty-four hours a day."

Only after an international campaign of public protests and decisive measures by the Cuban government to roll up a network of so-called dissidents in Cuba, organized and financed by the US government, did federal authorities return the Five to the general prison population a month later.

In subsequent years Hernández especially has been thrown in the hole multiple times. And like many other prisoners, the Cuban revolutionaries—especially the three in maximum-security institutions—have been subjected to prison lockdowns, in which all inmates are confined to their cells, often for several days, during which they are denied visitation rights and face other restrictions.

On top of the maximum sentences and harsh treatment, the Five have been denied the normal right to receive visits from their loved ones. Their wives, mothers, and children, who live in Cuba,

---

2. A recently declassified May 2004 memorandum from the US Justice Department to the Department of Defense advised that solitary confinement up to thirty days of prisoners at Washington's notorious Guantánamo Bay detention camp would not constitute "cruel, inhuman, or degrading" treatment under the Convention Against Torture and could thus be defended legally. But if the Defense Department "wished to extend that time," the memorandum said, the Justice Department "ought to be consulted again." The memo was written by Assistant Attorney General Jack L. Goldsmith III.

What conclusion is to be drawn about the six months that Hernández and Labañino were held in solitary confinement under the direct responsibility of that same "Justice Department"?

---

3. In September 2011, the US government declassified a May 13, 2003, letter from the State Department to Cuban diplomats at the Interests Section in Washington, DC, that sheds light on the timing of these punitive actions against the Cuban Five in early March 2003, as Washington was preparing its invasion of Iraq later that month. The letter pointed to "numerous examples of Cuban espionage against the United States." According to anonymous sources cited in a September 21, 2011, *Miami Herald* article, although the May 2003 letter didn't explicitly charge the Cuban government with having passed along information about US invasion plans to the Iraqi regime, that was a central purpose of the State Department's warning note.

have been able to visit only once a year on average because of the long delays in obtaining visas. And US authorities have outright denied all visa requests by Adriana Pérez and Olga Salanueva to visit their husbands, Gerardo Hernández and René González.

Stepped-up attacks on workers' rights

The frame-up of the Cuban Five—beginning with the 1995–98 FBI operation that led to their arrest—was carried out by the Clinton administration and its Justice Department, headed by Attorney General Janet Reno. US District Judge Joan Lenard, who presided over the November 2000–June 2001 trial, is herself a Clinton appointee.

Over this same period, the US capitalist rulers and their political representatives in both the Democratic and Republican parties were stepping up assaults on workers rights, as well as on the wages and social gains of working people.

In 1994 the government enacted the Violent Crime Control and Law Enforcement Act, which among other provisions undermined Fourth Amendment protections of "the right of the people to be secure in their person, houses, papers, and effects, against unreasonable searches and seizures." The law allowed prosecutors in some cases to use evidence in court that was obtained without a warrant. It allocated federal funds to put one hundred thousand more local cops on the streets.

The 1996 Illegal Immigration Reform and Immigrant Responsibility Act expanded the immigration cops' powers to seize and deport undocumented workers without the right to judicial review or appeal. The *migra* was expanded to become the largest federal police agency.

The Orwellian-named Anti-Terrorism and Effective Death Penalty Act of 1996 allowed immigration police to jail immigrants using evidence to which they and their attorneys were denied access. It broadened government powers to use wiretaps and hold an accused person in preventive detention without bail.

The government further restricted prisoners'

The frame-up of the Cuban Five was carried out as the US rulers stepped up their attacks on political rights. **Above:** Heavily armed immigration cops raid a Miami home in April 2000 to take six-year-old Elián González. The Clinton administration used that case to reinforce powers of the immigration police that are exempt from judicial review and—as with the Cuban Five—deal a blow to the constitutional right to be safe from arbitrary search and seizure.

appeal and parole rights. Mandatory "minimum" sentences and longer terms became more common, including life without parole.

The government expanded to some sixty the number of federal offenses punishable by death, and executions accelerated after the adoption of the 1994 Federal Death Penalty Act. The Comprehensive Terrorism Protection Act of 1995 denied the right of death row prisoners to submit more than one habeas corpus petition for federal court review of their cases.

Under the Clinton presidency, between 1993 and 2001, the number of people behind bars jumped by 42 percent. Lockdowns and solitary confinement were increasingly used. Today some 2.3 million people in the United States are behind bars—the highest per capita rate of incarceration in the world.

In 1999 the US government framed up Taiwanese-born scientist Wen Ho Lee, who was accused of stealing nuclear secrets for China. While the government was unable to prove a case of espionage, it denied him bail and held him in solitary confinement for nine months, using the case to strengthen its abrogation of rights in the name of "national security." In September 2000 all charges but a minor one were dropped and Lee was released.

In April 2000, heavily armed commandos of the Immigration and Naturalization Service (INS) raided a home in Miami to seize six-year-old Elián González from relatives who were holding him. The White House exploited its half-year-long refusal to return the child to his father in Cuba in order to burnish the image of the INS, reinforce the agency's powers that are exempt from judicial review, and deal a blow to the Bill of Rights, which guarantees US residents are safe in their homes from unreasonable searches and seizures. The Miami raid was conducted while the Cuban Five were in federal custody awaiting trial.[4]

The George W. Bush administration, inaugurated in January 2001, continued on the course set by the US ruling class. It seized on the Sept. 11, 2001, attacks to win passage of the Patriot Act and other laws to authorize expanded police wiretapping of phones, interception of electronic communications, and spying on political groups and individuals. The sentences against the Cuban Five were handed down in December 2001, as Washington escalated its "war on terror."

Under the banner of "homeland security," the government has sought to legitimize the use of "preventive detention" of terrorist "suspects" with no charges, courts closed to the public, and even torture, often referred to euphemistically as "enhanced interrogation." It is moving to try Guantánamo prisoners—including US citizens—in military tribunals where they would be denied constitutional protections.

Meanwhile, immigration cops have stepped up raids of factories and working-class neighborhoods, arresting, deporting, and sometimes bringing criminal charges of "identity theft" against foreign-born workers.

Because of the experiences by millions of workers and farmers with assaults on their constitutionally protected rights and their conditions of life and work—and the growing resistance to these attacks—the case of the Cuban Five strikes a chord among many who learn of it. Working people engaged in protests against immigration raids, police frame-ups, and other instances of class "justice" in the United States are the most responsive to appeals to support the campaign to free the Five.

By standing up, fighting, and extending a hand of solidarity to others, these five revolutionaries have themselves been in the front ranks of the class struggle in the United States.

JULY 14, 2008

---

4. In November 1999, Elián González, then five years old, was picked up at sea off the Florida coast after his mother and ten other passengers drowned during a smuggler-organized boat trip from Cuba. His father and the Cuban government demanded he be returned. The US attorney general's office, however, placed him in the custody of a distant relative in Miami. Right-wing forces in Miami held highly publicized demonstrations condemning the Cuban government and opposing the boy's repatriation. For seven months the Clin-

ton administration refused to return the child, in violation of Cuba's sovereignty. Meanwhile, hundreds of thousands in Cuba mobilized repeatedly in rallies, marches, and other actions to demand that Washington return him to his country, winning broad international support. On April 22, 2000, heavily armed immigration cops and US marshals seized Elián González in a commando-style raid on the Miami home. Two months later he was finally returned to Cuba.

WHY THE CUBAN REVOLUTION IS A BONE IN UNCLE SAM'S THROAT

By Martín Koppel

What was the supposedly criminal activity in which the Cuban Five were engaged?

They were keeping the Cuban government informed about the activities of US-based counterrevolutionary groups that have a long record of launching attacks on Cuba, most often from Florida.

The armed actions of those outfits are one front of the five decades of political, economic, and military aggression—carried out under eleven administrations, Democratic and Republican—through which the US government has sought to weaken and prepare the overthrow of the Cuban Revolution and reimpose capitalist rule.

Washington's goals are neither irrational nor dictated by short-term political or electoral calculations. The propertied families that rule the United States are determined to make the workers and farmers of Cuba pay for having the audacity to take state power and make a socialist revolution. From the beginning, what they have hated and feared above all is the political example this revolution sets for working people around the world, including right here in the United States.

"What is it that is hidden behind the Yankees'

BOHEMIA

August 1960 march in Havana with symbolic burial of coffins representing US-owned companies nationalized by the revolution. US capitalist rulers have waged fifty years of aggression against Cuba's socialist revolution because they fear its example worldwide.

hatred of the Cuban Revolution?" asked the Second Declaration of Havana, a manifesto adopted in February 1962 by a million-strong assembly of the Cuban people.

"What unifies them and incites them is fear," was the answer. "Not fear of the Cuban Revolution, but fear of the Latin American revolution. . . . fear that the plundered people of the continent will seize the arms from their oppressors and, like Cuba, declare themselves free peoples of the Americas."

Revolutionary measures

On January 1, 1959, workers and farmers in Cuba, led by the Rebel Army and July 26 Movement, overthrew the US-backed Fulgencio Batista dictatorship. The revolutionary government immediately began mobilizing working people and taking steps that were in their interests.

Within months it approved laws that reduced rents by 30 to 50 percent and slashed the onerous electricity and telephone service rates charged by the US-owned monopolies.

Racist discrimination in employment and public facilities was outlawed. Steps were taken to encourage women to become involved in the broad social struggles unfolding.

In May 1959 a sweeping agrarian reform was enacted, expropriating the largest landed estates and giving land titles to 100,000 landless peasants.

Free public education for all children was established, and health care was expanded to all social layers. In 1961 some 250,000 volunteers—including nearly 100,000 students, largely teenagers—mobilized throughout the country to teach 700,000 workers and peasants to read and write, wiping out illiteracy in less than twelve months.

Workers organized and mobilized to combat economic sabotage by the capitalist owners of factories and plantations. By the end of 1960, major US companies and virtually all large-scale Cuban-owned industries had been nationalized. To defend the revolution in face of escalating attacks by Washington and US-backed counterrevolutionary forces, workers militias were organized across the country.

These and similar measures established the socialist character of the revolution.

Cuba's revolutionary leadership extended its solidarity to anti-imperialist struggles around the world. As early as 1963 Cuban volunteer troops went to Algeria to defend the newly independent government there against an imperialist-backed assault. This proletarian internationalist course continues to this day, with thousands of Cuban vol-

JUVENTUD REBELDE

Cuban women's antiaircraft and antitank unit in Angola, 1988. Between 1975 and 1991, hundreds of thousands of Cuban volunteers helped defeat invasions of Angola by the apartheid regime in South Africa. Imperialist rulers fear the example of proletarian internationalism set by revolutionary Cuba.

unteer medical personnel providing quality health care throughout Africa, Latin America, and Asia.

These measures, making deep inroads on the prerogatives of capital, infuriated the US ruling class and wealthy Cuban property owners. Unlike other governments, Cuba's leadership was not beholden to their interests. Most alarming to them, revolutionary Cuba was setting a dangerous example to millions around the world—that working people are capable of overturning capitalist rule and reorganizing social relations in their interests.

In July 1960 Washington cut off virtually all sugar imports from Cuba. In January 1961 it broke diplomatic relations with Cuba and restricted travel by US citizens to the island. By February 1962 the John F. Kennedy administration ordered a total embargo on US trade with Cuba.

In April 1961, the White House organized an invasion of Cuba by 1,500 mercenaries, which workers and farmers, organized through their popular militias, Revolutionary Armed Forces, and revolutionary police, defeated at the Bay of Pigs in fewer than seventy-two hours.

In October 1962 Kennedy ordered a naval blockade of the island and brought the world to the brink of a nuclear holocaust after Cuba accepted missiles from the Soviet Union in face of Washington's preparations to invade Cuba.

US-organized terror campaign

Between 1959 and 1965, nearly four thousand counterrevolutionary bandits—armed, trained, and financed by the US government—waged a campaign of sabotage and terror, especially in the Escambray mountains of central Cuba. They tortured and killed hundreds of people, including literacy volunteers and peasants benefiting from and supporting the land reform. Cuban working people organized to defeat the counterrevolutionary bands, which they succeeded in doing by the mid-1960s.

Over the years US-backed terror squads burned sugarcane fields, bombed Havana department stores, and carried out hundreds of attempts to assassinate Fidel Castro. Cuban authorities have offered evidence that Washington has carried out biological warfare against the Caribbean nation, including introducing agents causing outbreaks of African swine fever in 1971 and hemorrhagic dengue fever in 1981.

In recent decades the US government has escalated its economic war against Cuba, including through the 1992 Torricelli Act and 1996 Helms-Burton Act, which among other things penalize non-US companies that do business with Cuba.

CIA-trained counterrevolutionaries also carried out murderous attacks on US soil and in the US colony of Puerto Rico. Eulalio Negrín, a Cuban American businessman who favored moves to normalize US-Cuban relations, was killed on November 25, 1979, in Union City, New Jersey.

Félix García Rodríguez, a diplomat at the Cuban mission to the United Nations, was killed on a New York street on September 11, 1980.

Carlos Muñiz Varela, a leader of the Antonio Maceo Brigade, was killed in San Juan, Puerto Rico, on April 28, 1979. The Brigade had been organized two years earlier by young Cubans living in the United States and Puerto Rico who identified with the Cuban Revolution and defended it against Washington's attempts to crush it.

In October 1976, CIA-trained counterrevolutionaries blew up a Cuban airliner over Barbados, killing all seventy-three people aboard, many of them teenage members of the Cuban fencing team. Among those implicated in the horrendous crime were Orlando Bosch and Luis Posada Carriles, who were arrested in Venezuela. Posada Carriles, formerly a mercenary at the Bay of Pigs, had worked as chief of operations for the Venezuelan secret police. He was allowed to escape from prison in 1985 before he had been tried.

In a 1998 *New York Times* interview, Posada Carriles bragged about his involvement in a series of bombings of Havana hotels in 1997, including one that killed an Italian Canadian visitor, Fabio Di Celmo, at the Hotel Copacabana. Posada Carriles was also implicated in a November 2000 failed assassination attempt in Panama against Fidel Castro. Today both Posada Carriles and Bosch walk freely in the streets of Miami.* Washington has refused the Venezuelan government's request for the extradition of Posada Carriles.

Brothers to the Rescue

One of the US-based Cuban American counterrevolutionary groups is Brothers to the Rescue, an out-

---

* Bosch died in Miami in April 2011.

fit that has falsely portrayed itself as a "humanitarian" group rescuing Cubans who leave the island on rafts. Its leader, José Basulto, trained by the CIA, was involved in the Bay of Pigs invasion and has a long history of armed attacks on Cuba.

Planes flown by Brothers to the Rescue pilots repeatedly violated Cuba's airspace, provocatively flying over the island and dropping leaflets calling on the Cuban people to revolt against the government. Cuban authorities report that Brothers to the Rescue conducted some twenty-five such illegal incursions between mid-1994 and February 1996, and on numerous occasions Havana filed protests with US authorities over these provocations. The protests were ignored.

On February 24, 1996, Basulto led three Cessna planes into Cuban airspace heading toward Havana. The pilots ignored unambiguous warnings by Cuban air traffic controllers to turn back. Cuban air force jets then shot down two of the planes with four Brothers to the Rescue members, while Basulto's plane got away. After that decisive action by Cuba to defend its sovereign territory, all provocative flights from the United States stopped.

In response to the shootdown, the Clinton administration stepped up its hostile actions against the Cuban Revolution. That included passage of the Helms-Burton Act less than a month later in March 1996, as well as the arrest and frame-up of the Cuban Five in September 1998.

The US government targeted one of the five,

Gerardo Hernández, for particular retribution. Hernández was sentenced to a second life term on a charge of "conspiracy to commit murder"—the unproven claim that he had been "supporting and implementing a plan" by the Cuban government to shoot down the Brothers to the Rescue planes in international waters.

In justifying their violent actions against Cuba, outfits like Brothers to the Rescue claim to speak for all Cuban Americans. But the Cuban population in the United States is not monolithic, either in class composition or political opinions.

The armed right-wing outfits represent the interests of only a small handful of wealthy businessmen, including the former capitalist tycoons of Cuba and their henchmen, who after 1959 lost their ability to exploit the workers and farmers of Cuba.

The large majority of Cuban Americans are working people, not capitalist property owners. Today, many if not most—especially among those who emigrated in recent decades, as well as the new generations born in the United States—oppose the economic war on the people of Cuba and the travel restrictions imposed by the US government, especially the limits on their right to visit their families on the island.

Some Cuban American organizations, such as the Alianza Martiana in Miami, speak out against these US policies and demand the release of the Cuban Five.

OCTOBER 20, 2008

WHO ARE GERARDO, ANTONIO, RAMÓN, FERNANDO, AND RENÉ?

By Martín Koppel

The five Cuban revolutionaries have defeated all attempts by their jailers to break them. They continue to tell the truth about the Cuban Revolution and the reasons for their frame-up by the US government. They continue to explain to fellow prisoners who they are. They continue to speak out in defense of all those everywhere, in the United States and around the globe, who are fighting for a world free of exploitation and oppression in all their forms.

In Cuba the Five are national heroes, held in the highest esteem for the volunteer mission they undertook and for continuing today to act as revolutionaries from behind US prison walls.

In the United States, as the economic crisis deepens and new working-class struggles break out, broader layers of working people and youth are finding out about the Cuban Five. In the heat of these battles, many come to see in them courage and dignity that is to be emulated.

Who are these men and what have they accomplished?

All five are exemplary products of Cuba's socialist revolution.

Gerardo Hernández Nordelo

Hernández, forty-seven, was born in Havana on June 4, 1965.[1] As a teenager he became a leader of the Federation of High School Students, joining the Union of Young Communists when he was in the eleventh grade. In 1989 he graduated from Havana's Higher Institute of International Relations, where he had been active in the Federation of University Students. In 1988 he married Adriana Pérez O'Connor, who worked at the Food Industry Research Institute.

On graduating Hernández, like many of his fellow students, volunteered to serve in Angola,

Gerardo Hernández in US prison in Victorville, California.

departing Cuba the day before his first wedding anniversary. Between 1975 and 1991, more than 375,000 Cuban volunteers served as internationalist combatants in that African country, helping the Angolan people defeat invasions by the South African apartheid regime.

A lieutenant, Hernández headed a scouting platoon in a tank brigade that helped defend Cabinda, a strategically important oil-rich region of Angola, from counterrevolutionary assaults. He distinguished himself in fifty-four missions, and was awarded medals for his outstanding record. Based on this record, and the esteem in which he was held by fellow combatants, he became a member of the Cuban Communist Party in 1993.

In a 2002 interview in the Cuban paper *Juventud Rebelde*, Urbano Bouza Suriz, who fought in Angola under Hernández's command, described his leadership qualities. "Twelve Cubans slept [in a small bivouac], and the fact that he, as an officer, shared both the good and the bad with his subordinates won him respect," Bouza noted. "We went out on reconnaissance almost every day. Sometimes at night we took part in ambushes around our

---

1. Ages listed in this article are as of September 2012.

unit." In his spare moments, Bouza commented, Hernández "read a lot, especially books by Che [Guevara]."

Hernández "was prepared from a political, human, and psychological point of view" for the US mission he subsequently undertook in the mid-1990s, said Bouza. "A scout must be an excellent observer, show confidence in face of danger, be discreet, courageous. I can see those qualities in Nordelo," as Hernández was called by his fellow combatants.

When he read in the press about Hernández's arrest and frame-up trial, Bouza said he told his neighbors with pride, "That was my leader in Cabinda!"[2]

Hernández is an accomplished cartoonist. His humorous drawings have been published since 1982, and in 2002 a book of his work was published in Cuba, *El amor y el humor todo lo pueden* (Love and humor can achieve anything).

Hernández is serving two life sentences plus fifteen years at the Victorville maximum-security federal penitentiary, located in the Mojave Desert in southern California. He has not seen his wife, Adriana, since before his arrest, as the US government has repeatedly denied her a visa to visit him.

Antonio Guerrero Rodríguez

Guerrero, fifty-three, was born into a working-class family in Miami on October 16, 1958. His father, who had moved to the United States seeking work as a professional baseball player, helped raise funds in Miami for the July 26 Movement and Rebel Army during the revolutionary struggle to overthrow the Batista regime. The family returned to Cuba for a visit in November 1958 and decided to stay after the revolutionary victory in January 1959.

In a July 2004 interview, Guerrero's sister María Eugenia, nicknamed Maruchi, said that, influenced by the example of their parents, "my brother and I had an active life in student organizations." Early on in school, she said, they became leaders of the José Martí Pioneers Organization of children, the Federation of High School Students, and the Union

Antonio Guerrero in US prison in Florence, Colorado.

of Young Communists.

After finishing high school Guerrero—known better as Tony—won a scholarship to study at the University of Kiev in Ukraine. He graduated there with top honors in civil engineering in 1983. On his return he worked on a major project to expand the runway at the Antonio Maceo International Airport in Santiago de Cuba.

In 1989 Guerrero became a member of the Cuban Communist Party. He worked for the national airline, Cubana de Aviación, as an airport construction specialist. He married a Panamanian citizen and lived in that country for a few years. Later he moved to Miami, working maintenance jobs at the Boca Chica naval air base in Key West.

Guerrero has two sons, twenty-seven-year-old Antonio and Gabriel, nineteen.

An artist and a poet, Guerrero has penned numerous poems in prison, a selection of which was published in English and Spanish under the title *From My Altitude*. In prison he learned to draw and paint from fellow inmates, and a collection of his artwork has been exhibited in cities throughout North America.[3]

He was sentenced to life plus ten years and locked up at the "supermax" federal penitentiary in Florence, Colorado. In October 2009 he won a reduction in his sentence to twenty-one years and ten months, and was moved to the Florence medium-security prison. In January 2012 he was transferred to the medium-security prison in Marianna, Florida.

2. See article in Part III, "'Twelve Men and Two Cats': With Gerardo Hernández and His Platoon in Angola."

3. See article by Guerrero in Part III, "Poet and Painter: Learning to Draw in Prison."

Guerrero told the federal courtroom at his sentencing in December 2001, "If I were asked once again to cooperate in this task, I would again do it with honor."

In an interview published in the September 2, 2008, issue of the Cuban magazine *Bohemia*, Guerrero said the Cuban Five should not be "viewed in a different dimension from millions of compatriots who each day give everything for the Revolution and who could have been in our place and would have acted in exactly the same way. We are nothing more than Cubans of these times, revolutionaries of these times."

Ramón Labañino Salazar

Labañino, forty-nine, was born in Marianao, Havana Province, on June 9, 1963, to parents of peasant origin. His mother Nereida was involved in support work for the Rebel Army in the eastern province of Oriente during the revolutionary war.

A student leader in high school, he studied at the University of Havana, majoring in economics. He also graduated at the top of his class from the university's five-year military training program. In 1987 Labañino joined the Union of Young Communists. The next year he took up duties as an officer of the Ministry of the Interior. In 1991 he became a member of the Cuban Communist Party, in which he came to hold leadership responsibilities.

A sports enthusiast, he practices karate and as a student took part in the All-Caribbean Games. He is married to Elizabeth Palmeiro, and has three daughters: Ailí, twenty-four; Laura, twenty; and Lizbeth, fifteen.

Ramón Labañino

As with his four imprisoned comrades, when Labañino moved to the United States in the early 1990s, he could not tell his wife or other family members about his assignment, not even when in 1998 he visited his critically ill mother, knowing he wouldn't see her again. "I never knew of the work he was doing," said his father, Holmes Labañino. "He never talked to me about it and I never asked. Since he was very young he has always known what to do and has always done the right thing."

Labañino told the courtroom on the day of his sentencing, "I will wear the prison uniform with the same honor and pride with which a soldier wears his most prized insignia. This has been a political trial; therefore, we are political prisoners."

Labañino was sentenced to life plus 18 years, and jailed for many years at maximum-security penitentiaries in Texas and later Kentucky. In December 2009 his sentence was reduced to 30 years, and he was then transferred to the medium-security prison in Jesup, Georgia.

Fernando González Llort

González, forty-nine, was born in Havana on August 18, 1963. He was a student leader in high school and college, as well as in the Union of Young Communists. He graduated with honors from the Raúl Roa García Higher Institute of International Relations.

Like tens of thousands of others of his generation, González volunteered for duty in Angola from 1987 to 1989. He was serving in a military intelligence unit there during the time that Cuban and Angolan troops defeated the South African apartheid regime's invading forces at the battle of Cuito Cuanavale. He was awarded the medals "Internationalist Combatant" and "For the Victory of Cuba—People's Republic of Angola."

In 1988, during his tour of duty in Angola, he was taken into membership in the Cuban Communist Party.

González has been with his companion Rosa Aurora Freijanes since 1990. Soon after they got together, he undertook his special assignment in the United States. "We had to go through endless red tape to marry in prison," said Freijanes in *Letters of Love and Hope*, a book of correspondence between the Cuban Five and their families.

Fernando González as volunteer combatant in Angola.

In the United States, González's main task was to keep CIA-trained counterrevolutionary Orlando Bosch under surveillance. Bosch was involved in the 1976 bombing of a Cuban airliner over Barbados that killed all seventy-three passengers and crew members.

González's mother Magali Llort describes her son as "a typical Cuban." She says he is "a man with ideas that have made him consistent, and with a loyalty to his country for which I think we should always be thankful."

In the statement he read before the federal court in Miami just before being sentenced in December 2001, he pointed to the US government's backing of counterrevolutionary murderers who attack Cuba. "As long as the situation remains as I have described it, Cuba has a moral right to defend itself in the way that my comrades and I have done," he said.

On learning about Fernando's dignified conduct during the frame-up trial, Bladimir La Rosa Vega, one of his fellow Angola combatants, told the Cuban press, "I honestly was not surprised to see his attitude."

González was given a nineteen-year sentence, which in December 2009 was reduced to seventeen years and nine months. He is currently locked up in the low-security federal prison in Safford, Arizona.

René González Sehwerert

René González, fifty-six, was born in Chicago on August 13, 1956. Like Antonio Guerrero, he is a US citizen. His father, Cándido González, a union

steelworker, and his mother, Irma Sehwerert, were active in the July 26 Movement among Cuban immigrant workers. After the 1959 revolutionary victory they remained in the United States to carry out work in defense of the revolution. In 1961 the family returned to Cuba, where René's parents became union leaders.

From an early age René González had wanted to become a pilot, but put off fulfilling his aspiration more than once to volunteer for other responsibilities. A cadre of the Union of Young Communists, he volunteered to work as a teacher in the countryside after graduating from high school.

Although as a dual citizen of the United States and Cuba he was exempted from military duty, he enlisted in 1974. He completed his military service with high grades as a tank driver.

In 1977, on his way to flight school, he learned that his former tank unit was going to Angola to join the internationalist mission there. González decided to join them.

Speaking at a 2003 meeting in Havana with youth from the United States, his mother Irma reported that at first René "was turned down because he had just completed his military service. He said, 'I have to go to Angola.' So he hopped on his bike on a Friday afternoon, pedaled several kilometers to find the two officials who could give him the necessary forms and signatures. He got the signatures. And early on Monday he left for Angola." He served in Angola until 1979 as a gunner in a tank brigade, and was decorated for bravery.

One of his fellow Angola combatants, Luis Nieves Otaño, later recounted that during their tour of duty, "the Cuban government publicly released the identities of several [Cuban state] security agents who had infiltrated the mafia-like groups based in the United States [and who by then had returned to Cuba]. After reading about it in a newspaper, we commented on the courage of those comrades, and I told René, 'You have the traits and the conditions to carry out such a mission.' He immediately replied, 'I hope so.'"[4]

After his return from Angola, González finally completed his training as a pilot. He worked as

---

4. See interview with González in Part III, "Angola Made Me Grow."

a flight instructor until 1985, when he was designated squadron chief at the air base in San Nicolás de Bari. In 1990 he became a member of the Cuban Communist Party. That same year he accepted his next mission in defense of the revolution—this time in the United States.

In his statement to the US court on his sentencing, he explained what the five were doing in Florida. "This issue of Cuban agents has a very simple solution: Leave Cuba alone. Do your job. Respect the sovereignty of the Cuban people," he said. "I would gladly say good-bye to every last spy who returns to the island. We have better things to do there, all of them a lot more constructive than watching the criminals who freely walk the streets of Miami."

René González was sentenced to fifteen years. He served most of his sentence at the US prison in Marianna, northern Florida. On October 7, 2011, he was placed on "supervised release" under the jurisdiction of the federal courts' probation office. US authorities are forcing him to remain in the United States for another three years under these conditions.

CUBADEBATE

René González on the day of his parole from prison, October 7, 2011, with father Cándido and daughter Irma.

René and his wife, Olga Salanueva, have two daughters, Irma, twenty-eight, and Ivette, fourteen. Salanueva, who was living with him in Miami at the time of his arrest in 1998, was deported to Cuba in 2000, her US residency revoked. She has not seen her husband in more than ten years.

NOVEMBER 24 AND DECEMBER 1, 2008

Where to write *Gerardo, Ramón, Antonio & Fernando*

Gerardo Hernández
Reg. #58739-004
US Penitentiary
P.O. Box 3900
Adelanto, CA 92301

**Ramón Labañino
(Luis Medina)**
Reg. #58734-004
FCI Ashland
P.O. Box 6001
Ashland, KY 41105
Note: *address envelope to "Luis Medina," but letter inside may be addressed to Ramón.*

Antonio Guerrero
Reg. #58741-004
APACHE A
FCI Marianna
P.O. Box 7007
Marianna, FL 32447-7007

**Fernando González
(Rubén Campa)**
Reg. #58733-004
FCI Safford
P.O. Box 9000
Safford, AZ 85548
Note: *address envelope to "Rubén Campa," but letter inside may be addressed to Fernando.*

THE 'MURDER CONSPIRACY' FRAME-UP OF GERARDO HERNÁNDEZ

By Martín Koppel

What happened on February 24, 1996, off the coast of Havana?

The facts help expose the US government's frame-up of Gerardo Hernández, who was convicted and sentenced to a double life term plus fifteen years on trumped-up charges, including "conspiracy to commit murder." Prosecutors accused Hernández of "supporting and implementing a plan" by the Cuban government to shoot down two hostile planes that invaded Cuba's airspace—the legitimate act of defense by a sovereign government.

On that day in 1996, three planes left Opa-locka airport near Miami and flew well into Cuban airspace. The planes were piloted by members of Brothers to the Rescue, a counterrevolutionary Cuban American group that for years had organized provocative flights over Cuban territory despite Havana's repeated warnings to Washington. This time, after they defied insistent warnings by Cuban air traffic controllers to turn back, two of the planes were shot down by Cuba's air force.

US officials, however, have tried to turn the victim into the criminal and the criminal into the victim. They claim Brothers to the Rescue was on a "humanitarian" mission to rescue Cubans drifting on rafts toward the shores of Florida. They assert the planes were downed in international, not Cuban, airspace. And they allege Hernández knew beforehand of a plan to shoot down the planes that day.

What are the facts?

Basulto's record: CIA-trained thug

Far from being a humanitarian, José Basulto, the founding leader of Brothers to the Rescue, is a CIA-trained counterrevolutionary. Questioned during his March 2001 testimony in the federal trial against the five Cuban revolutionaries, Basulto proudly acknowledged his decades-long record.

Basulto testified that after the victory of the Cuban Revolution he had been schooled by the CIA in Panama, Guatemala, and the United States. He "acknowledged that he was trained in intelligence, communications, explosives, sabotage and subversion," reported the March 13, 2001, *Miami Herald*. The CIA infiltrated him into Cuba, under the identity of a physics student at the University of Oriente in Santiago, to help prepare the ground for the 1961 US-organized mercenary invasion at the Bay of Pigs, which Cuban working people crushed in fewer than seventy-two hours.

In August 1962, Basulto and other counterrevolutionaries left the United States in a speedboat mounted with a 20-mm cannon, and fired from Cuban waters on the Sierra Maestra Hotel and the nearby Charles Chaplin (now Karl Marx) theater in Havana. In the 1980s he flew supplies to the *contras*, the US-organized and -financed

Gerardo Hernández (right) with attorney Leonard Weinglass.

military forces seeking to overthrow the Nicaraguan revolution.

Basulto, who became a well-off Miami businessman, said in the trial testimony that he launched Brothers to the Rescue in 1991 as a "humanitarian rescue" group to pick up Cubans seeking to reach Florida by raft. That was the cover under which the outfit carried out numerous provocative operations off Cuban shores—and reeled in millions in "nonprofit charity" donations.

Brothers to the Rescue shifted its tactics, however, after the 1994 and 1995 Cuba-US migration accords, under which federal authorities returned Cubans intercepted before reaching US shores. "Without rafters, the money dried up," said the *Miami Herald* reporting on Basulto's testimony.

And after February 24, 1996, it might be added, the volunteers dried up too.

Provocations against Cuba

Emboldened by Washington's lack of any action to prevent these provocations, Brothers to the Rescue stepped up its flights over Cuba in 1994. On November 10 that year the group flew two planes from the US naval base at Guantánamo and dropped leaflets over eastern Cuba calling on people to overthrow the government.

The outfit publicly acknowledged that in July 1995 and twice in January 1996 it organized flights that dropped antigovernment leaflets near Havana. The Cuban government repeatedly demanded that Washington take action to stop the incursions of its airspace. After a July 13, 1995, low-altitude flight over the capital city, Cuba issued a public warning that "any boats from abroad can be sunk and any aircraft downed" if they entered Cuban territory for hostile reasons.

Yet Washington did nothing—even the simple measure of revoking the pilots' licenses—to stop these escalating provocations.

On February 24, 1996, two hostile violations of Cuban airspace took place, Cuban authorities reported. In the first, three Cessna planes retreated after being intercepted by Cuban MiG fighter jets.

The second time, when the Havana air traffic control center detected one of the three Cessnas again heading toward Cuban airspace north of Havana, it issued a warning. The pilot, according to a Cuban foreign ministry statement, replied that

"it was clear he could not fly in that zone but he was going to do it anyway."

A transcript released by Washington, based on US intelligence recordings, contains the following radio exchange between the Havana air control tower and Basulto.

HAVANA: "We inform you that the area north of Havana is activated. You are taking a risk by flying south of 24 [the 24th parallel]."

BASULTO: "We are aware that we are in danger each time we fly into the area south of 24, but we are willing to do it as free Cubans."

The three planes penetrated Cuban airspace. After they ignored warning passes by the air force planes, two of the planes were shot down inside the island's twelve-mile territorial limit. The third plane, piloted by Basulto, fled back into international airspace.

Sovereign action in Cuban airspace

Washington has maintained that the shootdown took place in international airspace, although it acknowledged that Basulto briefly violated Cuban territory. The Clinton administration, as noted earlier, used this claim to justify passage of the Helms-Burton Act, a major escalation of economic war against Cuba.

In January 2001 Clinton signed an executive order giving $96 million in frozen Cuban funds to families of the four counterrevolutionaries killed in the shootdown. The money was seized from payments owed to Cuba's telephone company for phone services between the two countries.

US officials provided the International Civil Aviation Organization (ICAO) with radar data backing up their claim that the February 24, 1996, events took place over international waters. Radar data provided by Cuba, however, demonstrated that the Brothers to the Rescue planes were inside its territory.

A June 1996 ICAO report said the US and Cuban radar information could not be reconciled. It asserted nonetheless that the shootdown took place in international waters. The agency said it based its conclusion on the position of the US cruise liner *Majesty of the Seas*, which had been sailing near Cuba at the time.

The accuracy of the cruise ship's log, however, is a point of contention. The ICAO report itself acknowledges that "no corroborative evidence of the position of the *Majesty of the Seas* was obtained."

The ship's first officer, Bjorn Johansen, who testified for the prosecution in the trial of the Cuban Five, later told Brazilian researcher Fernando Morais he had based his reports on a "visual observation" of his ship's location, not the vessel's electronic register. Further tarnishing Johansen's credibility is the fact that the ship's owners, Royal Caribbean Cruise Line, were at the time major donors to the rightist Cuban American National Foundation, and Peter Whelpton, a company vice president, was a member of the foundation's "Blue Ribbon Commission for the Reconstruction of Cuba."

During the trial a defense witness, retired US Air Force Colonel George Buchner, questioned the ICAO findings and suggested that the only way to conclusively determine where the planes went down was to examine the US government's own satellite photos, which Washington refuses to release.*

He went on to say that the evidence showed the Brothers to the Rescue pilots were well inside Cuba's airspace when they were downed. Buchner, a former regional commander of the North American Air Defense Command (NORAD), said he had reviewed transcripts provided by the US National Security Agency of conversations between the MiG pilots and a Cuban commander on the ground. He concluded the two planes were shot down about 6 miles and 5.5 miles, respectively, off the Cuban coast.

"The trigger was when the first aircraft crossed the twelve-mile territorial limit," he testified. "That allowed the government of Cuba to exercise its sovereign right to protect its airspace."

In fact, Buchner said, the Cuban air force pilot "showed restraint" by breaking off pursuit of Basulto's plane as it got into international airspace.

Moreover, the *Miami Herald* reported, "Buchner said the Cessnas had given up their civilian status because they still carried the markings of the US Air Force and had been used to drop leaflets con-

demning the Cuban government."

Over the years, in fact, US-based counterrevolutionaries have used Cessnas and other "civilian" aircraft to conduct biological warfare on Cuban sugarcane and other crops, drop firebombs, and introduce saboteurs and spies on the island.

Shootdown not a 'plot'

Gerardo Hernández was charged with murder conspiracy for allegedly giving Cuban authorities information on the Brothers to the Rescue flight plan in February 1996, as part of a supposed plot to shoot down the group's planes.

In fact, Brothers to the Rescue itself had reported its flight plan to the Federal Aviation Administration (FAA), which then transmitted that information to the Havana air control authorities.

After months of escalating Brothers to the Rescue provocations and Cuba's warnings that these would not continue to be tolerated, both Washington and Havana were anticipating an incident. The day before the shootdown, an internal FAA memo warned that "it would not be unlikely that the [Brothers to the Rescue would] attempt an unauthorized flight into Cuban airspace tomorrow, in defiance of the government of Cuba and its policies" and that Havana "would be less likely to show restraint this time around."

Nor was the shootdown a surprise to Brothers to the Rescue leaders. Juan Pablo Roque, a former Cuban air force pilot who had gone to Miami in

US government did nothing to prevent counterrevolutionary group Brothers to the Rescue from repeatedly violating Cuban airspace prior to planes being shot down on February 24, 1996. **Above**: José Basulto, CIA-trained leader of the group who has a long history of violent actions against Cuba.

---

* In conjunction with Gerard Hernández's habeas corpus appeal, currently before the courts, his defense attorneys have also filed requests with US government agencies for copies of their satellite images of the area at the time of the shootdown. See also "Defense Attorney's Errors and New Evidence are Basis for Hernández Appeal" in Part II.

1992 and, posing as a counterrevolutionary had entered Brothers to the Rescue to monitor its actions, returned to Cuba the day before the shootdown. Appearing on Cuban TV three days later, Roque exposed some of the group's activities. This included, he said, plans to introduce antipersonnel ammunition into Cuba and blow up high-tension pylons to disrupt the energy supply.

In a February 27, 1996, CNN interview, Roque said he had told Basulto that Cuban authorities were expecting a provocation and were ready to shoot down intruding US aircraft.

"I tried to persuade Brothers to the Rescue not to continue their flights," he said. "But they would not listen. My opinion did not count, because they wanted martyrs to boost their anti-Castro industry."

AUGUST 3, 2009

> ## "Cuba has a moral right to defend itself the way that my compañeros and I have done."
> **Fernando González**
> December 2001

Right: Rally of 5,000 in Holguín, Cuba, November 19, 2011, demanding freedom for Cuban Five. It was organized by Federation of Cuban Women as part of international conference in support of campaign to free the Five.

EDGAR BATISTA/AHORA

EDGAR BATISTA/AHORA

Left: In front row of Holguín rally, from right: Rosa Aurora Freijanes and Elizabeth Palmeiro, wives of Fernando González and Ramón Labañino; Magali Llort (fourth from right) and Mirta Rodríguez (foreground), mothers of Fernando González and Antonio Guerrero. Roselia Taño, general secretary of Federation of Cuban Women in Holguín, is behind Rodríguez. Jorge Cuevas, Communist Party first secretary in province, is on far left.

RADHAMÉS MORALES

Right: April 21, 2012, demonstration in Washington, D.C., during five days of actions around the world to demand release of framed-up Cubans.

THE TRIAL OF THE FIVE: LESSONS IN CAPITALIST 'JUSTICE'

By Martín Koppel

From beginning to end, the federal trial in Miami of the five Cuban revolutionaries was a lesson in how the US "justice" system serves the ends of capitalist rule.

Defense requests to change the trial venue from Miami were repeatedly denied. The court severely restricted defense access to evidence introduced by the prosecutors. Although the government failed to prove its allegations of "conspiracy to commit espionage" and other charges, the five men were found guilty on all counts and given maximum sentences.

The proceedings, held in federal court in the Southern District of Florida, were a political trial from start to finish. Lasting nearly seven months, from November 2000 to June 2001, it heard seventy-four witnesses, including three retired US generals and a retired admiral. Despite the major issues it posed, from violations of rights guaranteed by the first ten amendments to the US Constitution—the Bill of Rights—to Washington's foreign policy, the proceedings received virtually no coverage in the US big-business media outside southern Florida.

FISA vs. the Bill of Rights

The government's case against the Cuban Five was built on "evidence" collected through wiretapping phone conversations and seizing computer files and other personal belongings from their homes. These actions were carried out by FBI agents, acting under the Foreign Intelligence Surveillance Act (FISA).

Signed into law by President Carter in 1978, FISA is designed to circumvent constitutional guarantees against warrantless searches and seizures and violations of due process. The act established a court that operates behind closed doors, inside the Justice Department, to authorize federal cop agencies to conduct physical and electronic surveillance in order to collect "foreign intelligence information."

US District Judge Joan Lenard rejected defense motions to suppress evidence obtained through these "unreasonable searches and seizures" barred by the Fourth Amendment to the Constitution. The court also allowed the prosecution to use documents collected in this manner while denying the same access to them by the defendants.

After federal agents seized more than 20,000 pages of materials from the five men, the Justice Department stamped every page "top secret." Not a single one, however, was a secret US government document.

The government then invoked the Classified Information Procedures Act (CIPA), under which the court restricted defense access to the evidence. The prosecutors were allowed to introduce heavily censored documents or "summaries" of documents as evidence. The defense attorneys could only review even the censored materials in a special room in the courthouse basement and were prohibited from taking their working notes from the facility.

A large amount of evidence was suppressed. Under the CIPA provisions, prosecutors met privately with the judge to decide what evidence would be kept from the defense and excluded from the trial. This included documents that could have contradicted the government's case.

For example, the prosecution alleged that Hernández had advance knowledge of the Cuban government's downing of the two Brothers to the Rescue planes. As proof, they asserted that after the shootdown, "Hernández wrote to his superiors that he and others took pride in having contributed to an operation that 'ended successfully'" and that Cuban intelligence commended Hernández for "outstanding results achieved on the job," as a US government brief argued.

In an April 1, 2009, phone interview with filmmaker Saul Landau published in *Progreso Weekly* magazine (reprinted in the July 20, 2009, *Militant*), Hernández explained how the evidence had been manipulated by suppressing documents.

Just before the shootdown, Hernández had helped Juan Pablo Roque, a fellow Cuban revolutionary who was working inside Brothers to the Rescue, return to Cuba. "The US government wanted to show that Roque's return was linked with the shootdown. That's absolutely false," Hernández said in the interview. "It's well documented that Roque's return had been planned for a year before that happened."

But the prosecution, he said, "cleverly removed from the evidence certain communications referring to Operation Venice—Roque's return—and made it seem that they referred to Operation Scorpion, the operation to stop the violation of Cuban airspace.

"One clear example is a message I sent responding to a request from Cuba saying that for me it was an honor to have made a modest contribution to a successful mission. It is super clear in the evidence that this referred to Operation Venice, the one about Roque. The government used it as its sole piece of evidence that I had something to do with the shootdown, although they know it did not refer to Operation Scorpion. . . . The prosecution mixed the two up purposely."

The US government also prevented the court-appointed defense attorneys from adequately preparing for the trial by limiting access to their clients, who were held in isolation cells for seventeen months prior to the trial.

Judge denies change of venue

From the outset, a central issue was the defense request for a change of venue on the grounds that the accused could not receive an impartial trial in Miami-Dade County. Despite the widespread publicity surrounding the arrests and trial and intimidating actions organized by Cuban American counterrevolutionary forces, Judge Lenard rejected seven defense motions to move the proceedings to another location, even to Fort Lauderdale in Broward County, just thirty miles to the north.

From the moment of the arrests, US officials whipped up an effort to convict the five in the media, announcing the discovery of a "Cuban spy network" in Florida that "threatens national security." The capitalist press in Miami did its part with sensationalist headlines and editorials about "Spies among us." *

Armed right-wing Cuban American groups, while much weaker than they were in earlier decades, were part of the picture. They organized protests in Miami during the trial, including actions marking the anniversary of the shootdown. In the months before the trial, Miami was also polarized by the controversy over Elián González, with rightists staging street protests opposing the return of the child to his father in Cuba.

During jury selection, several potential jurors admitted they were concerned about the repercussions if they acquitted the five Cubans. According to court records, David Cuevas, for example, said he would "fear for my own safety" if he didn't return a guilty verdict "acceptable to the Cuban community." Jess Lawhorn, a mortgage banker, expressed concern about economic reprisals that could "affect his ability to grant loans." Prospective juror John McGlamery said that because of publicity and the volatile atmosphere it could be difficult to follow the court's instruction not to expose oneself to information about the case.

These and similar portions of the trial record were later cited by the appellate court in sustaining the defense argument that the Five had been denied due process by the Miami court's refusal to grant a change of venue and order a new trial.

The concerns of many potential jurors were well-founded. On November 27, 2000, the first day of jury selection, right-wing forces organized a demonstration on the courthouse steps, featuring relatives of the downed pilots from Brothers to the Rescue. Jurors were exposed to the lunchtime protest, and some were approached by the press.

---

* See article in Part II, "Government-Paid Journalists Stoked Bias in Cuban Five Trial." It explains the role of the US government's Office of Cuba Broadcasting in paying thousands of dollars to journalists in Miami who wrote prejudicial articles about the five—one of the grounds for the habeas corpus appeals currently before the courts.

Judge Lenard took a few steps to give the appearance that jurors were insulated from such pressures. She instructed government officials to talk to the Brothers pilots' relatives about their improper conduct. She extended a gag order to cover jurors and witnesses in addition to attorneys, and sealed the jury selection questions. She ordered marshals to accompany jurors as they left the building. During the trial she also limited the sketching of witnesses for their protection.

Jurors continued to complain they felt harassed. The judge again modified their guarded transportation to the courthouse and entry and exit from the building.

But during deliberations, right-wing TV stations continued to film jurors entering and leaving the courthouse, all the way to their cars. Even their license plates were filmed.

At one point in the trial, when José Basulto, head of Brothers to the Rescue, was questioned by defense attorney Paul McKenna about that group's record of armed attacks on Cuba, Basulto shot back, "Are you doing the work of the intelligence service of Cuba?"—a clear warning to jurors of how they might be treated if they issued a verdict of not guilty.

The judge told the jury to ignore the remark and chided Basulto, but allowed the proceedings to continue.

Double standard

Federal prosecutors insisted from the beginning that an impartial trial for the five Cuban revolutionaries could be held in Miami-Dade County. Just one year later, however, in a separate case, *Ramírez v. Ashcroft*, US Attorney Guy Lewis—who had served on the prosecution team in the trial against the Cuban Five—moved for a change of venue in that proceeding on the basis that a fair trial in Miami-Dade was "virtually impossible" because of media coverage and community "prejudice."

In *Ramírez*, then-attorney general John Ashcroft and the Immigration and Naturalization Service were accused of employment discrimination against Latinos. In asking for a change of venue, the government cited many of the same facts it had previously dismissed as irrelevant in the case of the Cuban Five, including the right-wing demonstrations around the Elián González case.

During jury selection for the trial against the Cuban Five, a number of the twelve people chosen for the jury—which included no Cuban Amer-

MILITANT PHOTOS BY JONATHAN SILBERMAN

October 7, 2008 demonstration at US embassy in London calls for release of Cuban Five. **Inset:** Olga Salanueva (left) and Adriana Pérez, wives of René González and Gerardo Hernández, respectively, joined nighttime protest. The US government has repeatedly denied them a visa to visit their husbands. Protesters demanded that Washington grant them visas.

icans—expressed hostility toward the Cuban government. David Buker, who said he believed "[Fidel] Castro is a communist dictator and . . . I would like to see him gone and a democracy established in Cuba," was seated on the jury and named its foreman.

At the same time, the prosecution used its allotted peremptory challenges (those not requiring a reason) to strike African Americans from the jury. It used nine of its eleven peremptory challenges to strike potential jurors. Seven of the nine were Black. Subsequently, one of the grounds for appeals of the frame-up of the Cuban Five was that the disproportionate exclusion of African Americans from the jury was discriminatory, a violation of the Equal Protection clause of the Fourteenth Amendment to the Constitution.

Federal prosecutors had good reason to try to minimize the number of Blacks on the jury. From their own life experiences, many African Americans in southern Florida, especially workers, are more likely than others to smell a frame-up and bridle against the class bias of the cops and their "justice." And some have knowledge of revolutionary Cuba's outstanding contributions to liberation struggles worldwide.

2005 and 2006 appeals court rulings

On June 8, 2001, the US District Court convicted the five men on all counts of the federal grand jury indictment. In December Judge Lenard sentenced them to maximum prison terms. They were sent to five separate federal prisons around the country. Their attorneys appealed.

Nearly four years later, in August 2005, a three-judge panel of the Eleventh US Circuit Court of Appeals in Atlanta unanimously reversed the convictions and ordered a new trial.

Citing many of the facts already detailed in this article, the judges ruled that ensuring "an impartial jury in this case" was "an unreasonable probability because of pervasive community prejudice" in the Miami area. They pointed to "the media's publicity regarding 'The Spies Among Us'" and "the perception that these [counterrevolutionary Cuban] groups could harm jurors that rendered a verdict unfavorable to their views." And the government added fuel to the fire with inflammatory statements during closing arguments that the appeals court called "improper prosecutorial references."

The justices ruled that a new trial, in a different venue from Miami, was mandated by "the perfect storm" created by these conditions.

The US government challenged the appellate court decision and, in an infrequently used recourse, demanded a full (*en banc*) court review. In August 2006, in a 10 to 2 ruling, the appeals court in Atlanta reversed the panel's decision. It affirmed the trial court's denial of motions for change of venue and upheld the convictions. The remaining issues under appeal were sent back to the three-judge panel.

In a dissenting opinion, justices Stanley Birch and Phyllis Kravitch, who had served on the three-judge panel, reaffirmed their conclusion that the case warranted "a change of venue because of pervasive community prejudice" and the "convictions should be reversed and the case should be remanded for a new trial."

AUGUST 17, 2009

'The Five are in prison for all of us, for all those fighting for their dignity, their future, their liberation'

"Having reviewed the case extensively over a number of years, the organization believes that there are serious doubts about the fairness and impartiality of their trial. . . . Amnesty International is supporting calls for a review of the case by the US executive authorities through the clemency process or other appropriate means."

Amnesty International, October 2010 report

"The continued holding of the so-called Cuban Five is unwarranted. There have been doubts expressed in the US courts and among human rights organizations around the world. They've now served more than twelve years of imprisonment, and my hope is that in the near future they will be released to come back to their homes."

James Carter, former US president, March 30, 2011

"At one time it was the five Nationalists, five Puerto Rican brothers. Today it's five Cuban brothers. Back then, Cuba fought hard to win our unconditional release. Today the Cuban Five are in prison for us. For all men and women fighting for their dignity, for their future, for their liberation."

Rafael Cancel Miranda, Puerto Rican independence fighter,
one of the five Nationalist prisoners who spent 25 years in US prisons, February 2005

"The climate of bias and prejudice against the accused in Miami persisted and helped to present the accused as guilty from the beginning. . . . It proved almost impossible to select an impartial jury in a case linked with Cuba."

United Nations Working Group on Arbitrary Detentions,
five-judge opinion issued May 27, 2005

"On behalf of 3.3 million members, I am writing to protest the continued imprisonment of the Cuban 5 and to ask you [President Obama] to intervene so as to procure their release from prison. . . . They were in the US to monitor the activities of Cuban exiles who, operating from bases in Miami, were planning violent actions against innocent people in Cuba. The continued incarceration of these Cuban patriots is morally indefensible."

Kenneth Georgetti, president, Canadian Labour Congress, July 2012

"Our Cuban brothers played a decisive role in our struggle for Angola's independence. We are not going to stand there and do nothing while they remain in prison today. We will continue to fight for their freedom."

Luzia Inglês, general secretary,
Angolan Women's Organization, September 2008

The frame-up charges against the Cuban Five and their sentences

Gerardo Hernández, Ramón Labañino, Antonio Guerrero, Fernando González, and René González were convicted by a US federal court on June 8, 2001, on a total of 33 counts among them. They were given maximum sentences. Below are the charges against each and the sentences each was given by federal judge Joan Lenard in Miami.

GERARDO HERNÁNDEZ

- Conspiracy to murder

- Conspiracy to gather and transmit to a foreign government information relating to national defense (often shortened to "conspiracy to commit espionage" in court documents)

- Acting, and causing others to act, as an agent of a foreign government without registering with the Attorney General (7 counts)

- Conspiracy to act as an agent of a foreign government without registering with the Attorney General

- Fraud and misuse of documents (2 counts)

- Possession with intent to use five or more fraudulent identification documents

Hernández was sentenced to two life terms plus fifteen years. In 2008 a federal appeals court ruled that his life sentence for conspiracy to commit espionage exceeded federal sentencing guidelines since no top secret information was gathered or transmitted. The court, however, refused to reduce the sentence on grounds that his other life term made the sentencing error "irrelevant to the time he will serve."

RAMÓN LABAÑINO

- Conspiracy to gather and transmit information relating to national defense

- Acting, and causing others to act, as an unregistered agent of a foreign government (4 counts)

- Conspiracy to act as an unregistered agent of a foreign government

- Fraud and misuse of documents (2 counts)

- Making a false statement in a passport application

- Possession with intent to use five or more fraudulent identification documents

Labañino was sentenced to life in prison plus eighteen years. In 2008 a federal appeals court ruled that his life sentence for conspiracy to commit espionage exceeded federal guidelines since no top secret information was gathered or transmitted. In 2009 the sentence was reduced to thirty years, followed by five years of supervised release.

ANTONIO GUERRERO

- Conspiracy to gather and transmit to a foreign government information relating to national defense

- Acting as an agent of a foreign government without registering with the Attorney General

- Conspiracy to act as an unregistered agent of a foreign government

Guerrero was sentenced to life in prison plus ten years. In 2008 a federal appeals court ruled that his life sentence for conspiracy to commit espionage exceeded federal guidelines since no top secret information was gathered or transmitted. In 2009 the sentence was reduced to twenty-one years and ten months, followed by five years of supervised release.

FERNANDO GONZÁLEZ

- Acting, and causing others to act, as an agent of a foreign government without registering with the Attorney General (2 counts)

- Conspiracy to act as an unregistered agent of a foreign government

- Fraud and misuse of documents

- Possession with intent to use five or more fraudulent identification documents

Fernando González was sentenced to nineteen years in prison. In 2008 a federal appeals court ruled that his sentence exceeded federal guidelines since he did not have control or supervisory responsibility over other defendants in regard to the false ID charge. In 2009 the sentence was reduced to seventeen years and nine months, followed by three years of supervised release. His prison release date is February 27, 2014.

RENÉ GONZÁLEZ

- Acting as an agent of a foreign government without registering with the Attorney General

- Conspiracy to act as an agent of a foreign government without registering with the Attorney General

René González was sentenced to 15 years in prison, followed by three years of supervised release. After 13 years and 24 days in prison, he was paroled in October 2011 and is serving his supervised release in Florida.

PART II

'We Will Continue Until Victory'

Freedom will be won by "a jury of millions."

Gerardo Hernández, September 2008

Top left: New York City, June 29, 2009, picket line at Federal Building.

Top right: Washington, D.C., march on September 13, 2008. Holding banner are Róger Calero, Socialist Workers Party 2008 presidential candidate, and SWP leader Mary-Alice Waters.

Middle left: Davis, California, some 75 youth, mostly Chicano, discuss Cuban Five case at a forum at University of California campus sponsored by Sigma Lambda Beta fraternity, May 6, 2009.

Middle right: Los Angeles, speakers at August 13, 2011, event for Cuban 5. From left: Alicia Jrapko, International Committee for the Freedom of the Cuban Five; Tony Woodley, former general secretary of Unite union in United Kingdom; Cristina Vázquez, international vice president of Service Employees International Union (SEIU); Mike García, president of SEIU-United Service Workers West; and Natasha Hickman, editor of *Cuba Sí*, publication of Cuba Solidarity Campaign in United Kingdom.

Bottom: Minneapolis, opening of "Humor from My Pen" exhibit of political cartoons by Gerardo Hernández, November 19, 2011.

APPEALS COURT UPHOLDS CONVICTIONS, ORDERS THREE SENTENCES REDUCED

By Sam Manuel

A federal appeals court in Atlanta on June 4, 2008, denied an appeal by five Cuban revolutionaries to overturn their unjust convictions, nearly ten years after they were locked up by the US government on frame-up charges.

The three-judge panel, however, vacated the sentences against three of the men, two of whom are serving life terms. It sent their cases back to the original trial judge for resentencing on the basis that the prison terms were excessive.

This was the second appeal by Antonio Guerrero, Gerardo Hernández, Ramón Labañino, Fernando González, and René González to reach the appellate court. In 2005 a three-judge panel of the same court, the Eleventh US Circuit Court of Appeals, threw out the convictions on the basis that the five men did not get a fair trial in Miami. A year later the full twelve-judge court reversed that ruling, while allowing for appeals on other points to go forward.

In the June 4, 2008, ruling, one of the three judges, Stanley Birch, supported upholding the convictions but at the same time reiterated his belief that the defendants did not receive a fair trial in Miami and that their request for a change of venue should have been granted and a new trial ordered in the earlier appeal. "The defendants were subjected to such a degree of harm based upon demonstrated pervasive community prejudice that their convictions should have been reversed," he wrote. During the 2001 trial, Judge Joan Lenard had rejected repeated defense motions for moving the trial out of Miami, where right-wing threats and widespread media bias created a prejudicial atmosphere.

The five were convicted on charges of conspiracy to gather and transmit information related to national defense, failing to register as agents of a foreign government, and other frame-up charges. Hernández was also falsely accused of "conspiracy to murder."

The National Lawyers Guild, in a statement protesting the ruling, quoted Leonard Weinglass, an attorney for the Cuban Five, who noted, "Conspiracy has always been the charge used by the prosecution in political cases." That way the government doesn't have to prove that espionage actually happened but can impose sentences (in the case of Gerardo Hernández two life terms plus fifteen years) as if espionage had actually happened, Weinglass noted.

To sustain a conspiracy charge, the government must prove the existence of "an agreement to achieve an unlawful objective" but not that "the defendants accomplished the purpose of the conspiracy," the ruling said in upholding the conviction of René González, who is serving fifteen years.

Dissent on 'conspiracy to murder'

The judges were split 2–1 in upholding the conviction of Gerardo Hernández on the charge of conspiracy to commit murder. The charge was in connection with the 1996 shootdown by the Cuban air force of two planes flown by Brothers to the Rescue, a Cuban American rightist outfit that over the years had repeatedly violated Cuban airspace in increasingly aggressive actions. Its leader, José Basulto, has a long history of armed attacks against Cuba, including his involvement in the 1961 US-organized mercenary invasion of Cuba at the Bay of Pigs and an assault on a Cuban hotel in 1962.

René González and another Cuban, Juan Pablo Roque, who was not in the United States at the time of the arrests, had joined Brothers to the Rescue to obtain information on its plans for overflights and possible attacks against Cuba. The US government alleges that on instructions from Havana, Hernández had told the two men to avoid flying with the group during a range of dates on which the Cuban air force would "confront" the provocative flights.

Prosecutors also cited alleged remarks by Hernández after the shootdown expressing approval of the self-defense action taken by the Cuban government. These two things, it said, constituted an "agreement" or "conspiracy" by Hernández in relation to the shootdown.

In a strongly worded sixteen-page dissent, Judge Phyllis Kravitch voted to overturn Hernández's conviction, calling the government's evidence "speculation" at best. She noted that Brothers to the Rescue had repeatedly violated Cuban airspace since 1994, flying low over downtown Havana on one occasion. The Cuban government, she wrote, twice filed written complaints with the US Federal Aviation Administration about the incursions, warning that Cuba had the right to down any invading aircraft. Basulto even appeared on Miami radio boasting of the flights, but US authorities took no action against him.

The judge noted that a conspiracy charge must be based on agreement to "achieve an unlawful objective," but that the US government failed to prove that Hernández's goal was "to shoot down the planes in international, as opposed to Cuban, airspace." The Cuban government says it shot down the planes within its own airspace.

Kravitch added that the government "failed to provide sufficient evidence that Hernández entered into an agreement to shoot down the planes at all."

Disproportionate sentences

On the basis of this unfounded charge, Hernández was sentenced to a double life term plus fifteen years. René González was sentenced to fifteen years, Fernando González to nineteen years, Ramón Labañino to life plus eighteen years, and Antonio Guerrero to life plus ten years.

While upholding the convictions of all five, the court was unanimous in ruling that the sentences for Labañino, Guerrero, and Fernando González were excessive and had no basis in the law. It found that the government failed to show that Labañino or Guerrero had transmitted any "top secret" documents to Cuba, and failed to prove that González was a "manager" of the group.

Constitutional rights violations

The government's case against the Cuban Five is built on "evidence" taken secretly from their homes and computers by FBI agents under the Foreign Intelligence Surveillance Act (FISA). Under that 1978 law—an attack on protections guaranteed by the first ten amendments to the US Constitution, the Bill of Rights, against unreasonable searches and seizures—a secret court was set up inside the US Justice Department to rubber-stamp requests by federal cop agencies to spy on US residents without having to apply for a warrant at a regular court.

The June 4 ruling upheld the trial court's decision not to exclude evidence obtained under the secret searches, stating that the government had certified that the request approved by the FISA was proper. "When, as here, the applications contain the required certifications, they are subject 'only to minimal scrutiny

Picket line in San Francisco June 6, 2008, after Atlanta appeals court upheld conviction of Cuban Five.

by the courts.' The reviewing court has no greater authority to review the certifications of the executive branch than the FISA court has."

The ruling upheld trial judge Lenard's decision to bar the defendants and their attorneys from viewing the full documents presented as evidence, on the basis that some documents might contain classified information. Defense attorneys were allowed to view heavily censored documents or "summaries."

Attorneys for the Cuban Five say they will ask the full court to reconsider its ruling. They said they are also considering an appeal to the US Supreme Court.

JUNE 23, 2008

'DEFENDANTS' CONVICTIONS SHOULD BE REVERSED'

"Despite the district court's numerous efforts to ensure an impartial jury in this case, we find that empaneling such a jury in this community was an unreasonable probability because of pervasive community prejudice. . . .

"The government's arguments regarding the evils of Cuba and Cuba's threat to the sanctity of American life only served to add fuel to the inflamed community passions. . . .

"A new trial was mandated by the perfect storm created when the surge of pervasive community sentiment, and extensive publicity both before and during the trial, merged with the improper prosecutorial references."

—from August 2005 decision by justices Stanley Birch, Phyllis Kravitch, and James Oakes, three-judge panel of US 11th Circuit Court of Appeals in Atlanta that overturned convictions of Cuban Five and ordered a new trial

"This case is one of those rare, exceptional cases that warrants a change of venue because of pervasive community prejudice making it impossible to empanel an unbiased jury. . . . The defendants' convictions should be reversed and the case should be remanded for a new trial."

—from dissenting opinion by justices Birch and Kravitch, August 2006, when 12-member federal appeals court in Atlanta reversed 2005 ruling and upheld convictions

"The government failed to present evidence sufficient to prove beyond a reasonable doubt that Hernández agreed to participate in a conspiracy, the object of which was to shoot down BTTR [Brothers to the Rescue] planes over international airspace. . . .

"I would reverse the conviction and sentence with regard to Count 3, conspiring to commit murder."

—from dissenting opinion by justice Kravitch, June 2008, when three-judge panel of federal appeals court in Atlanta upheld convictions of the Five but overturned sentences of Labañino, Guerrero, and Fernando González

SUPREME COURT REFUSES TO HEAR APPEAL
Actions Demand: 'Free Five Cubans in US Jails!'

By Seth Galinsky

The US Supreme Court on June 15, 2009, refused—without comment—to review the case of the Cuban Five. Supporters of the five Cuban revolutionaries responded to the decision by holding picket lines in several cities and are stepping up efforts to win the Five's freedom.

"Based on the experience that we have had, I am not surprised by the Supreme Court decision," Gerardo Hernández said from prison in a statement released by Cuba's National Assembly. "There are no longer any doubts that our case has been from the beginning a political case."

Attorneys for the five had filed the appeal with the Supreme Court on January 30. Twelve *amicus curiae*—friend of the court—briefs were submitted to the court, backing the request that the case be reviewed.

Among those filing the briefs were the Mexican American Political Association, National Lawyers Guild, National Conference of Black Lawyers, Civil Rights Clinic at Howard University School of Law, and ten Nobel Prize winners.

The briefs take up three main aspects of the more than six-month-long trial in 2001: the refusal of the trial judge to grant a change in venue despite pervasive anti-Castro prejudice in Miami, the dismissal by government prosecutors of seven potential jurors who are Black, and the conviction of Hernández without any evidence of conspiracy to commit murder.

The National Lawyers Guild and the National Conference of Black Lawyers note in their brief that on the very first day of jury selection anti-Castro rightists held a press conference and packed the courtroom.

Similar intimidation occurred throughout the trial.

In August 2005, the three-judge panel of the Eleventh Circuit Court of Appeals ruled that the sentiment against the Cuban Revolution among many in Miami, "extensive publicity both before and during the trial," and "improper" statements by the prosecutors combined to create a "perfect storm" that made a fair trial for the five impossible. The court ordered a new trial. Its decision, however, was overturned a year later by the full twelve-judge court.

In refusing to review the case the Supreme Court "did what the Obama administration requested of it," the Cuban National Assembly stated after the decision was announced. "We see manifested once more the arbitrariness of a corrupt and hypocritical system."

"Now is the time to step up our actions and not leave one leaf unturned or one door unopened" in the fight to free the Five, the assembly said.

Thirty people joined a picket line in front of the White House soon after the decision was announced, shouting "Justice delayed is justice denied! Free the Cuban Five now!"

The protesters demanded that President Barack Obama pardon the Five. Other protests were held in San Francisco and New York City.

"As long as one person remains struggling outside, we will continue resisting until there is justice," Hernández emphasized in his statement.

Susan LaMont in Washington, DC, contributed to this article.

JUNE 29, 2009

SENTENCE REDUCED FOR ANTONIO GUERRERO

Government Hears 'Noise' of International Condemnation

By Mary-Alice Waters and Ernest Mailhot

MIAMI, October 13, 2009—Antonio Guerrero left a Southern District of Florida federal courtroom today with a reduced sentence of twenty-one years and ten months. With time off for his record of conduct, acknowledged in the ruling by US District Judge Joan Lenard, Guerrero now has the possibility of parole in some seven years. When Guerrero walked into the courtroom earlier in the day, he was serving a sentence of life imprisonment plus ten years with no possibility of parole, handed down by the same judge in December 2001.

Guerrero and the other four Cuban revolutionaries have been held in US prisons since 1998 on a variety of trumped-up charges, including conspiracy to commit espionage and conspiracy to murder. In June 2008 a federal appeals court vacated the sentences for three of the Five—Guerrero, Ramón Labañino, and Fernando González—ruling the sentences were excessive because they were inconsistent with the court record. The appeals court ordered that each of the three be resentenced.

In the case of Guerrero and Labañino, the appeals court ruling noted they had been convicted of conspiracy to engage in espionage, yet no evidence had been introduced that they had actually gathered or transmitted any top secret information to the Cuban government.

In addition to the reduced sentence and possibility of parole for the first time, there is also a reasonable possibility coming out of today's hearing that Guerrero will be assigned to a medium-security federal correctional institution instead of a maximum-security penitentiary, such as the one in Florence, Colorado, where he has been confined since 2002. [Since January 2012 he has been held at the medium-security prison in Marianna, Florida.] As Guerrero's attorney Leonard Weinglass noted in addressing the court today, lockdown time at the federal penitentiary in Florence has averaged 30 percent!

In handing down today's decision, the federal court rejected arguments by both the lead government lawyer, Caroline Heck Miller, and Guerrero's attorney, Leonard Weinglass, in favor of a prehearing agreement they had reached to propose to the judge reducing Guerrero's sentence to twenty years. That would have been one year and ten months less than the federal guidelines for the trumped-up charges on which Guerrero was convicted. Instead, Lenard imposed the minimum sentence within the federal guidelines, which are advisory to judges, but not mandatory.

Lenard pressed Caroline Heck Miller—who was also the federal government's lead attorney at the time of the 2001 trial of the Five, where she had argued vigorously for a life sentence—to explain the government's reasons for proposing a penalty below the minimum statutory sentencing guidelines.

Alluding to the effectiveness of the international campaign in defense of the Five, Miller noted that the case has been surrounded by great "contentiousness and noise" and that the government was in favor of "giving something up" in order to try to "quiet the waters of contentiousness that swirl around this case worldwide."

What better reason to step up that international campaign demanding freedom for the Cuban Five!

OCTOBER 26, 2009

FERNANDO GONZÁLEZ AND RAMÓN LABAÑINO WIN REDUCED SENTENCES
Government Acknowledges There Was No Espionage

By Mary-Alice Waters and Ernest Mailhot

MIAMI, December 8, 2009—Ramón Labañino walked into a Southern District of Florida courtroom here today throwing a broad smile and thumbs-up sign to more than forty supporters who were present, and blowing a kiss to his wife Elizabeth Palmeiro, who was seated in the front row. Both Labañino and fellow defendant Fernando González entered and exited their respective court appearances today with similar dignity and gestures, exuding confidence that despite their more than eleven years in US federal prisons, the campaign to win their freedom is gaining strength worldwide.

In June 2008 a federal appeals court vacated the sentences for three of the Cuban Five—Antonio Guerrero, Labañino, and Fernando González—

Ramón Labañino visited by his father Holmes and his brother Holmito at McCreary federal prison in Kentucky, April 2010.

ruling the sentences were inconsistent with the court record. The appeals court ordered that each of the three be resentenced.

In the case of Guerrero and Labañino, the court ruling noted they had been convicted of conspiracy to commit espionage, but "the district court did not find that top secret information was gathered or transmitted." The life sentences they were given in December 2001 by Federal District Judge Joan Lenard were therefore inconsistent with federal sentencing guidelines.

In the case of Fernando González, the Court of Appeals ruled that there was no finding that he "asserted control or influence" over any other participant in "the crime." For that reason the sentence of nineteen years was excessive. Their cases were sent back to Lenard for resentencing.

Labañino, who had been serving a life sentence plus eighteen years (with no possibility of parole), left the courtroom today with his sentence reduced to thirty years. González's sentence of nineteen years was reduced to seventeen years and nine months. On October 13 Antonio Guerrero's sentence of life plus ten years had been reduced to twenty-one years and ten months.

The Court of Appeals refused to vacate the draconian double life plus fifteen years sentence given Gerardo Hernández, or the fifteen-year sentence given to René González. One of Hernández's life sentences was imposed on the same erroneous grounds as Guerrero and Labañino's life sentences. The appeals court, however, ruled that "Hernández need not be resentenced because the errors . . . are harmless." Hernández was also sentenced to life imprisonment on a trumped-up murder-conspiracy conviction related to the shooting down of two airplanes violating Cuban airspace in February 1996. The appeals court ruled that "any error in the calculation of Hernández's concurrent sentence for conspiracy to gather and transmit national-defense information is 'irrelevant to the time he will serve in prison.' "

The reduction of Labañino's sentence to thirty years—the minimum within the advisory federal sentencing guidelines—was recommended by attorneys for the US government and by defense attorney William Norris. The recommendation was accepted by Lenard at the conclusion of a brief hearing.

In the case of González there was no recommendation from attorneys for the two sides, and Caroline Heck Miller, assistant US attorney for the Southern District of Florida, introduced a lengthy summary of testimony and documents presented in the 2001 trial. She attempted to rationalize the government's position that the seriousness of the threat to US national security represented by González's action merited the longest sentence possible. She was answered by defense attorney Joaquín Méndez.

The five Cuban defendants, as they have reiterated over and over again in the course of their fight for freedom, were in the United States at the request of the Cuban government to monitor the activities of ultraright Cuban American organizations in Florida and to provide advance warning to the Cuban government of violent attacks planned on Cuban targets. Prosecutor Miller, however, described them as agents of a foreign government carrying out "acts of vigilantism on US soil." She called for the harshest possible sentence to be given to González as a "deterrent" against "all foreign agents."

Miller said the conduct of the Cuban Five is "celebrated by a foreign government, providing a powerful incentive to others" to engage in similar activity within the United States. She said that needed to be met with "a powerful disincentive." She was referring to the fact that in Cuba the Five are national heroes whose names and faces are seen everywhere, and that a worldwide campaign for their freedom continues to gain momentum.

During the resentencing hearing for Guerrero two months earlier, Miller had acknowledged the heat the US government feels as a result of the broad international support that has been won for the five. In response to the judge's questions, Miller told the court that the government hoped the reduced sentences would calm the "contentiousness" and "noise" swirling around the case.

As Judge Lenard imposed a barely reduced sentence on Fernando González, she echoed the arguments advanced by the US government attorney referring to acts of "vigilantism by a foreign government." Lenard said that "foreign governments have to know that such activities will not be tolerated" in the United States. She called attention to the recent "tragedy at Fort Hood"* and said that "protection of the constitutional rights of citizens and safety of US military installations and personnel" was fundamental to the national security interests of the country.

As a statement by Antonio Guerrero, Ramón Labañino, and Fernando González released to the press immediately after today's hearings makes clear (see accompanying article), the reduced sentences that have now been won for three of the defendants place all in a stronger position to step up the fight for the freedom of the five.

DECEMBER 21, 2009

Fernando González at US prison in Terre Haute, Indiana.

---

* A reference to the killing of thirteen US soldiers at Fort Hood, Texas, November 5, 2009. Major Nidal Malik Hasan, an army psychiatrist who is Muslim and of Palestinian descent, has been charged in the killings. A trial, scheduled for March 2012, has been postponed.

CUBAN FIVE: 'WE WILL CONTINUE UNTIL VICTORY'

The statement below was distributed to the press following the December 8, 2009, hearing in Miami to resentence Fernando González and Ramón Labañino.

Dear sisters and brothers of Cuba and the world:

We have now served more than eleven years in prison without justice being done in any part of the process that we have been through in the US judicial system.

Three of us were transferred to Miami to be resentenced by order of the Eleventh Circuit Court of Appeals of Atlanta, which determined that our sentences had been erroneously imposed.

Our brother Gerardo Hernández, who is serving two life sentences plus fifteen years in prison, has been arbitrarily excluded from this resentencing process. His situation continues to be the primary injustice of our case. The US government knows the accusations against him are false and that his sentence is unjust.

This has been a complex process, thoroughly discussed in every detail, in which we participated together with our lawyers. We have not given up even one iota of our principles, honor, and decency, always defending our innocence and the dignity of our homeland.

Just like when we were arrested, and on other occasions during these long years, this time we have also received proposals from the US government to collaborate in exchange for more benevolent sentences. And once again we reject such proposals, something that we will never accept under any circumstances.

The work of the legal team and the indestructible solidarity of all of you is present in the results of these resentencing hearings.

It is a significant fact that the US government, for the first time in eleven years, was forced to recognize that we caused no damage to its national security.

Also for the first time the prosecutors publicly acknowledged the existence of a strong international movement in support of our immediate freedom that is affecting the image of the US judicial system in the eyes of the international community.

Once again, the absolutely political character of this process is confirmed.

We the Five are being punished for accusations that have never been proven. Although three of our sentences have been partially reduced, the injustice against all of us has been maintained.

Meanwhile the Cuban American terrorists continue to enjoy total impunity.

We reiterate: The Five are innocent!

We are deeply moved and thankful for the ongoing solidarity that you have given us and that is so decisive in this long battle for justice.

Together with all of you we will continue until the final victory, which will only be achieved with the return of the Five to the homeland.

Antonio Guerrero Rodríguez
Fernando González Llort
Ramón Labañino Salazar
DECEMBER 21, 2009

CUBA PRESSES FIGHT FOR RETURN OF RENÉ GONZÁLEZ

By Michel Poitras

René González, one of the five Cuban revolutionaries serving draconian sentences in US prisons, was released October 7, 2011, after serving more than thirteen years of his fifteen-year term. On September 16, US District Judge Joan Lenard rejected González's motion that he be allowed to return to Cuba and serve in his own country a three-year supervised release that is part of his sentence.

His motion, filed in February of this year, is based on grounds that he has no close family in the US and his wife, Olga Salanueva, has been repeatedly denied a visa by Washington to visit him.

Lenard ruled that a decision on González's motion was "premature" prior to a period of experience with the "supervised release."

González's attorney, Philip Horowitz, explained in a phone interview September 27 that the conditions of González's release, including where he lives, are in the hands of the US Probation Office.

In recent weeks, the high-stakes battle to win the release of all five Cubans has received unusual public attention.

During a September 7–14 trip to Havana, Bill Richardson, former governor of New Mexico, presented a White House offer to waive probation for González in exchange for agreement by the Cuban government to release Alan Gross, a US citizen serving a fifteen-year sentence in Cuba for distributing sophisticated satellite equipment as part of a covert State Department operation to undermine the Cuban government.

Cuba rejected Richardson's proposition after he described Gross to the press as a "hostage" of Cuba and arrogantly vowed to stay in Cuba until he met Gross. "Cuba is a sovereign country which does not accept blackmail, pressure or posturing," stated Josefina Vidal of Cuba's Foreign Affairs Ministry. Judge Lenard's decision not to waive her instruction that González serve his probation in the US came two days after Richardson's trip. González's request had been sitting on her desk since February.

In an interview with *New York Times* editors and reporters published September 23, Cuban foreign minister Bruno Rodríguez Parrilla responded to questions concerning the release of Gross saying, "I can tell you the agenda submitted [for discussion] to the US government—and I reiterate here it is still on the table—included the topic of the Cuban Five, although we understand that as it is an element related to justice, it is also of a humanitarian character."

"I do not see any way in which we can move on toward a solution of the Mr. Gross case but from a humanitarian point of view and on the basis of reciprocity," Rodríguez added.

In an earlier interview with the *Militant*, defense attorney Horowitz stressed that defendants with dual citizenships, like González who is both a US and Cuban citizen, are often allowed to serve their parole outside the United States.

González has offered to renounce his US citizenship following his release if there were agreement he would be allowed to return to Cuba that same day.

OCTOBER 10, 2011

DEFENSE ATTORNEY'S ERRORS AND NEW EVIDENCE ARE BASIS FOR APPEAL BY HERNÁNDEZ

By Michel Poitras

Gerardo Hernández is one of five Cuban revolutionaries held in US prisons since 1998 who have filed habeas corpus motions in federal court to vacate their 2001 convictions and sentences on trumped-up conspiracy charges. With the Supreme Court two years ago having refused to hear all appeals by Hernández and his four compañeros, the habeas motions are the remaining legal option in the fight to reverse the frame-up and win their freedom.

Hernández's conviction on murder conspiracy charges stems from the US government's effort to connect him to the February 24, 1996, action by the Cuban air force shooting down two planes that had entered Cuban air space. The four pilots died. The flights were staged from US soil by Brothers to the Rescue, a Miami-based counterrevolutionary organization that had repeatedly violated Cuban air space despite Havana's formal protests to Washington and warnings about the consequences.

In his October 12, 2010, habeas corpus petition, Hernández argues that his conviction and sentence should be vacated, among other reasons, because he did not receive a proper defense at his trial.

In an April 25, 2011, response, Washington's attorneys opposed Hernández's habeas motion and request for an evidentiary hearing where he could present new information. They argued that the court at the time of the trial had "appointed experienced criminal counsel, Paul McKenna, who ably defended [Hernández] with great energy, loyalty, diligence, and professional skill, easily surpassing the minimal threshold for effective assistance of counsel."

This is not McKenna's opinion, however, as he explained in an Aug. 15, 2011, affidavit in support of Hernández's habeas motion. "Hernández's trial was more complicated than any other case I have ever tried," wrote McKenna, "involving unusual facts, novel questions of law, and very high profile proceedings."

McKenna went on to explain why Hernández's conviction and sentence should be overturned. "I never considered," he wrote, nor discussed with his client, "the possibility of filing a motion on Hernández's behalf to sever [the conspiracy to commit murder charge] from the remaining allegations against him."

A separate trial, explained Hernández in a March 16, 2011, affidavit, would have allowed him to testify on his own behalf without being compelled to present testimony regarding the other charges he and his codefendants faced. Hernández would also have been able to call on one or more of his codefendants to testify in a separate trial,

Gerardo Hernández, one of the Cuban Five prisoners, 2008.

without foregoing their Fifth Amendment protection against self-incrimination.

"Had I known that, I would have insisted that my lawyer make every effort to secure a separate trial on that count," Hernández emphasizes in his affidavit. He goes on to describe in detail how he would have testified to rebut evidence used against him by prosecutors.

McKenna says in his affidavit that at the time of the trial he acted on the belief "that if I could show that the shootdown had occurred in Cuban airspace, my client would have a viable defense" to the conspiracy to commit murder charge because it was "a justifiable act by the Cuban government."

"I now believe that my decision to pursue this line of argument—which was impossible to prove as a factual matter, and of questionable relevance as a legal matter—resulted in my client's conviction, as our presentation undermined our credibility and focused the jury on the actions of the Government of Cuba," McKenna wrote.

In fact, as Hernández's current lawyer, Richard Klugh, explained at a September 12, 2011, press conference, McKenna never pursued the line of defense that could have led to an acquittal—simply that "Gerardo was never involved" in the downing of the planes.

Finally, McKenna wrote in his affidavit that during the trial he had acted on the belief that "the Court was going to issue an instruction stating that the Government was required to prove that my client had intended for the shooting to occur over international waters, a burden of proof that the Government acknowledged was 'insurmountable.'"

Miami Meeting Defends Cuban Five

MILITANT PHOTOS BY DEAN HAZLEWOOD

MIAMI—Eighty people gathered here September 18, 2011, for a meeting in solidarity with the Cuban Five, organized by the Alianza Martiana, a coalition of Cuban American organizations opposed to US policy toward Cuba. The decision by Judge Joan Lenard that René González must remain in the United States following his release from prison October 7, means this is a "new moment of commitment" for all supporters of the fight, said Andrés Gómez, inset, president of the Antonio Maceo Brigade. Also speaking were Max Lesnik, president of the Alianza Martiana, and Elena Freyre of the Foundation for Normalization of US/Cuba Relations. September 12 through October 6 was set by supporters of the Cuban Five as a period of concentrated activity worldwide to call attention to the case.

—NAOMI CRAINE

But McKenna wrote in his affidavit that while the trial was under way he did not catch the fact that the judge did not issue such an instruction, and instead instructed the jury only regarding the murder and conspiracy charges.

"My errors at, before, and during the trial," McKenna wrote, "allowed the Government to convict my client even though it had no direct evidence of criminal intent on his part."

At the September 12 press conference, Klugh stated that McKenna's "very candid recognition" that Hernández did not receive the competent defense he had a right to provides a strong argument for setting aside his conviction and life sentence.

Mary-Alice Waters contributed to this article.

OCTOBER 3, 2011

GOVERNMENT-PAID JOURNALISTS STOKED BIAS IN CUBAN FIVE TRIAL

By Michel Poitras

One of the current fronts in the legal fight by the Cuban Five to overturn their frame-up convictions exposes the fact that some of the journalists who wrote false and inflammatory articles about the case during their trial in Miami were at the time on the US government payroll.

Four of the five Cuban revolutionaries have filed habeas corpus motions based on the fact, unknown to them and their lawyers at the time of the trial, that the government paid thousands of dollars to journalists in Miami who produced fictitious and prejudicial articles that deprived them of their right to due process and a fair trial.

In September 2006 the *Miami Herald* published a front-page article headlined "10 Miami Journalists Take U.S. Pay," reporting for the first time that well-known reporters in the Miami area who covered the case, including some who wrote for the *Miami Herald* and its Spanish-language edition *El Nuevo Herald*, had received payments from the US government's Office of Cuba Broadcasting, an arm of the Broadcasting Board of Governors, the government agency in charge of all nonmilitary international broadcasting sponsored by the US government.

The Office of Cuba Broadcasting directs the operation of Radio and TV Martí—two government stations funded to the tune of some $30 million a year that transmit counterrevolutionary propaganda in Cuba and southern Florida.

According to the reply filed August 16, 2011, by Guerrero to the government's response to his habeas motion, journalist Ariel Remos received at least $11,750 during the trial, publishing at least fifteen articles both before and during the proceedings in *Diario las Américas*, a Spanish-language daily with a circulation of more than forty-five thousand in southern Florida. In a concocted story titled, "Castro Represents a Continuous Challenge to the Security of the US," Remos falsely reported from the trial that there was a so-called "order of the Cuban intelligence service to one of its agents to find a place in south Florida to unload explosives and weapons," which, the article asserted, "could be chemical or bacteriological weapons."

According to information obtained from the government under a Freedom of Information Act request by the National Committee to Free the Cuban Five, Julio Estorino worked for Radio Martí from 1998 to 2001, although payments for his service during the trial have not been disclosed.

In the Jan. 5, 2001, issue of *Diario las Américas*, more than a month after the trial began, Estorino wrote: "For if the insanity shown in the downing of the airplanes from Brothers to the Rescue over international waters, with cold, malicious calculation, were not enough, now it comes to light that Castro's secret services have been trying to find infiltration points for weapons and explosives on the coastlines of this country, a task that was assigned to some of those implicated in the spy network."

A habeas corpus motion arguing for a new trial on the basis of the government's payment to journalists was filed by lawyers for Antonio Guerrero in late March 2011. In response the government urged the court to reject the motion on the grounds that it cites only a small number of articles and lacks a "factual basis" because it does not show how those articles prejudiced the jury, which the "Court took steps to insulate from outside influences."

As affidavits filed by the defendants document, the scope of Washington's propaganda campaign is unknown because US officials have denied freedom of information requests for the names of all the journalists on its payroll and the amounts paid.

The limited information obtained from the government shows that five journalists received more than $80,000 during the seven-month trial and that a total of some $370,000 has been paid to seven reporters at various times since 1999.

Violation of constitutional rights

The arrest and trial of the Cuban Five was marked by what have become increasingly common violations of rights guaranteed by the first ten amendments to the US Constitution, including FBI burglaries of their homes, the use of secret "evidence" by the prosecution and suppression of evidence for their defense, and the use of extreme pretrial solitary confinement in an attempt to break them and impede the preparation of their defense.

The trial court denied seven motions from lawyers for the five that the trial take place somewhere other than Miami-Dade County, where they faced a particularly biased atmosphere. Washington vehemently opposed all efforts to change the venue.

In fact, from the moment of the arrests, US government spokespersons promoted public hostility by issuing statements about the five being a "Cuban spy network" that "threatens national security." Despite being much weaker than they had been in the past, right-wing Cuban American groups known for their violent actions against those deemed even sympathetic to the Cuban Revolution organized protests in Miami during the trial, including on the courthouse steps during the first day of jury selection.

TERRY COGGAN/MILITANT

Protesters outside US consulate in Auckland, New Zealand, demand release of Cuban Five, June 12, 2008.

Potential jurors said they were concerned about what could happen if they acquitted the Cuban revolutionaries. During the trial, jurors complained they felt harassed as right-wing TV stations filmed them entering and leaving the courthouse, all the way to their cars, even filming their license plates.

"Just as the government was contending that the trial should go forward in Miami," said Richard Klugh, an attorney for Hernández, at a March 22, 2011, press conference, it was "flooding the local media with money to fund anti-Cuba, anti-Castro, anti-Cuban Five messages. That was a fundamental denial of due process."

In 2005, a three-judge panel of the Eleventh Circuit Court of Appeals in Atlanta threw out the convictions of the five revolutionaries on the grounds that "the 'perfect storm' created by pretrial publicity surrounding this case" denied them due process, and ordered a new trial. The government appealed the ruling, which was then reversed a year later by the full twelve-judge panel of the same court, with one judge strongly dissenting.

The 2006 ruling stated: "Nothing in the trial record suggests that twelve fair and impartial jurors could not be assembled by the trial judge to try the defendants impartially and fairly."

The habeas motions are before Judge Joan Lenard, who presided over the 2001 trial. On the basis of the 2006 ruling, government prosecutors made a case in their response to Hernández's habeas motion that the question of the trial venue has already been settled, that there's nothing new worth considering. They urged the judge to dismiss the habeas motions and deny requests for evidentiary hearings.

A habeas corpus motion was filed by Fernando González September 11. Once all motions, affidavits, and replies have been filed, the timing of her ruling is at the judge's discretion. [On December 6, 2011, government prosecutors responded to motions by González and Ramón Labañino, saying the claims "lack merit" and "fail to show (the two Cubans) suffered any prejudice."]

Mary-Alice Waters contributed to this article.

OCTOBER 10, 2011

US GOVERNMENT ATTORNEYS DISCLOSE 2010 PRISON VISIT BY OLGA SALANUEVA

By Louis Martin and Doug Nelson

Recently released court documents concerning requests by Cuban revolutionary René González to return to his country now that he has served his prison term in the US illustrate one fact clearly—Washington remains determined to impose the highest possible price on the men and women of Cuba who have made and continue to defend a socialist revolution ninety miles from US shores.

After more than thirteen years in prison, González was released October 7, 2011. He has since been forced to remain in the US on a three-year term of "supervised release" under surveillance of the federal probation office.

In February 2011 attorneys for González filed an initial request that he be allowed to return to Cuba upon his release and serve his parole there. That motion was rejected in September 2011 as "premature" by US District Judge Joan Lenard, the original trial judge.

On June 22, 2012, González's attorney, Philip Horowitz, filed a new motion for his return to Cuba. On July 16 US government attorneys asked Lenard to reject that request as well, and Horowitz filed a July 30 reply to the government's arguments.

Forcing González to remain in the US not only continues to keep him isolated from his family, defense attorney Horowitz pointed out. It also exposes him to danger of reprisal by forces hostile to the Cuban Revolution. A recent death threat against González on a Miami radio call-in program was cited as evidence.

González is required to notify every new acquaintance of his legal status, which would reveal his identity, Horowitz explained. This has imposed an extraordinary isolation as he "cannot befriend his most immediate neighbors, or even establish any form of casual friendship."

González has been unable to obtain a driver's license because the state of Florida requires that he reveal his address. Even his "access to health care was remarkably and unexpectedly much higher in prison than it could ever be under the current conditions."

Isolation from their families has been part of Washington's policy of maximizing the punitive conditions imposed on the Cuban Five from the beginning.

In González's case, his wife, Olga Salanueva, their two daughters, and his parents all live in Cuba. In November 2000, on the eve of the trial against the five, the US government deported Salanueva to bring pressure on González. Subsequently US officials declared her to be "permanently ineligible" to enter the country and have denied every visa application.

The recent court documents for the first time make public the fact that Salanueva was allowed to visit González in prison on one occasion—in November 2010, under terms of a special "accommodation." The visit, defense attorney Richard Klugh told the *Militant*, was "more traumatic than normal."

The affidavit filed by Horowitz points out that it occurred "under the most burdensome conditions." While Salanueva "was permitted to travel with her children, they were kept separated during her visit." She "was confined to a hotel under armed guard, and was able to see her husband briefly only before being sent back to Cuba."

The visit was part of a "confidential diplomatic accommodation" between the US and Cuban governments "in exchange for a family visit of an American prisoner being held in Cuba," a reply on behalf of González explained. The agreement to "keep this matter private" was broken by US

René González, Olga Salanueva, and their daughters, Irma (left) and Ivette (right), during his brief visit to Havana, April 2012.

government attorneys in court documents filed in March 2011, opposing González's request to return to Cuba following his release. They cited the visit as evidence González was not being prevented from seeing his wife. The March 2011 affidavit by the prosecution attorneys was not made public at the time.

"The fact that a prison visit was granted should not be used to block his rights post-release to be with his family," defense attorney Klugh told the *Militant*. This represents an unprecedented "violation of human rights standards."

Government attorneys themselves made clear the punitive nature of González's supervised release, Klugh said, when they "even opposed the defendant's request to visit his dying brother in Havana." The federal court granted the request over their objection. In April, González was allowed to spend two weeks in Cuba to see his brother Roberto, who died of cancer two months later.

The "American prisoner" being held in Cuba referred in the court documents above is Alan Gross, a contractor for the State Department's Agency for International Development who was arrested in Cuba in 2009 while on his fifth trip there in a year to install specialized satellite communications equipment for selected individuals. He is now serving a fifteen-year sentence for "acts against the territorial independence or integrity of the state." His wife, Judy Gross, was permitted to visit him in August 2010. The couple were given the privacy of a house for themselves alone at Tarará beach for a weekend.

Government attorneys argue González's request to serve the remainder of his parole in Cuba is essentially a request to "terminate" it. Such a motion can't be considered before serving at least "one year." They insist, moreover, his full compliance with the conditions of parole does not amount to the "exceptionally good behavior" the courts look for.

Because González is a US citizen—he holds dual citizenship—he should serve his parole in the US, the government attorneys assert. They reject as "unenforceable" offers by González to renounce his US citizenship if he is allowed to return to Cuba. He has declined to renounce it before returning to Cuba as he would be reimprisoned and held for deportation proceedings during an indefinite time.

Among the government's chief arguments is the fact that González was "resolutely and expressly unrepentant during and following his trial." In its brief, the government twice quoted from what they refer to as González's "vitriolic sentencing statement, and his explicit insistence on the right to continue to improve the world as he sees fit."

"I can only feel proud to be here and I can only thank the prosecutors for giving me this opportunity to confirm that I am on the right path and that the world still has a lot of room left for improvement," González said at his sentencing on Dec. 14, 2001. "I would like to believe you will understand why I have no reason to be remorseful."

Judge Lenard, who imposed the original sentence, will rule on the request that he be allowed to return to Cuba.

AUGUST 27, 2012

'MY YEARS IN THE UNITED STATES TAUGHT ME ABOUT CAPITALISM'

By Olga Salanueva

In the following interview, Olga Salanueva, the wife of René González, recounts some of her experiences as an immigrant worker in the United States, where she lived and worked for four years before being deported back to her native Cuba. Her story is one that millions of workers in the United States, immigrant and non-immigrant alike, will identify with.

In December 1990 René González, an experienced pilot and flight instructor, flew a "stolen" crop duster from Cuba to Key West, Florida, where he was welcomed by US authorities and other opponents of the revolution as a "Cuban defector." He joined the counterrevolutionary Brothers to the Rescue operation when it was formed the following year. González collected intelligence on the group's plans for actions against Cuba, which included, among other things, increasingly provocative flights into Cuban airspace and dropping leaflets over Havana.

In September 1998, FBI agents arrested González and his four fellow revolutionaries. Charged with failure to register as an agent of a foreign government and conspiracy to act as an unregistered foreign agent, he was sentenced to fifteen years plus three years of "supervised release."

In August 2000, as the case of the Cuban Five was about to go to trial, federal cops arrested Salanueva, threatening to revoke her permanent resident status and deport her. It was a clear attempt to coerce González into testifying against his four comrades. Unable to break him, US officials made good on their threat and deported Salanueva.

Since her deportation, Washington has denied each and every application by Salanueva for a visa to see her husband, accusing her variously of being a threat to US "national security," a Cuban intelligence agent, or even an individual tied to "terrorism." In 2008 US officials declared her "permanently ineligible" for a visa. Salanueva lives in Havana with their two daughters, Irmita, twenty-eight, and Ivette, fourteen.

In April 2012, Federal Judge Joan Lenard in Miami allowed González to return to Cuba for two weeks to visit his brother Roberto, who was terminally ill and died of cancer two months later.

Together with the wives, mothers, sisters, children, and other relatives of the five imprisoned revolutionaries, Olga Salanueva has been a tireless campaigner in the international fight to free the men, speaking on platforms across Cuba and around the globe.

The interview was conducted February 12, 2012, in Havana by

PRENSA LATINA/SINAY CÉSPEDES MORENO

Olga Salanueva (right) and Magali Llort, mother of Fernando González, speaking in Caracas, Venezuela, September 2011.

Mary-Alice Waters, Róger Calero, and Martín Koppel. The translation is by the *Militant*.

✍

MARY-ALICE WATERS: Olga, let's start by you telling us when you first arrived in the United States, and under what conditions.

OLGA SALANUEVA: I arrived on December 28, 1996. René is a US citizen because he was born there, so he was able to sponsor me and our daughter, Irmita, to gain legal residence.

René had left for the United States in 1990. After six long years of separation, we were happy our family was reunited and we could resume our plans, including having another child. Along with that happiness, however, I began a difficult, unforgettable stage in my life.

As with many immigrants, before I could enter the United States René had to sign an affidavit saying he would take responsibility for my expenses, that I wouldn't become a "burden to society."

It's ironic, but when you are sponsored by a US citizen and immigrate to the United States through legal channels, you don't get the help that Cubans who arrive on a motorboat receive under the so-called Cuban Adjustment Act.[1]

If you come on a small boat with no documents, the US government provides you job offers, health coverage for a year, and money to live on. That's only for Cubans, of course.

I knew no English and was on my own to find a job. We lived in Kendall, in southwest Miami. I didn't have much luck at first. The employment office told me I wasn't qualified. That I didn't know the language. That all they had were jobs for men—construction jobs and such.

Selling burial plots in Miami

WATERS: What did you study in Cuba?

SALANUEVA: I have a degree in industrial engineering and I also studied accounting. But in the United States they don't recognize your degree. You're required to get a certificate of equivalency, for which you first have to learn English. You

René González in Marianna federal prison in Florida in 2008 during visit by his daughters Ivette (left) and Irmita.

virtually have to start all over. I did take an accounting course and a computer science class to improve my chances.

My first job was in a nursing home, caring for the elderly residents who needed help. It was a private business, of course. I lasted three days. When René saw the conditions there—the dirty clothes, urine-soaked sheets, and long hours I worked—he said, "Let's get you out of there."

Then I saw an ad for a telemarketing job with a funeral home and got hired. They'd give us a list of telephone numbers and we'd call them, one by one, to sell funeral services: wakes, cremations, burials, burial plots.

I learned that in the United States, in what they call a "democracy," you must have money—or get it any way you can—so at the end of your life your remains can have a final resting place, without it becoming an added burden on your family.

When we made the phone calls, we were supposed to convince people to set an appointment for a salesperson to visit them. You had to get a certain number of appointments or they'd fire you.

It was a part-time job. We had no rights, no health insurance, and no vacations.

Most of the workers were Latinos. Some of the young women who worked with me had come from Cuba on rafts. Several told me they had made a mistake and were sorry they had left Cuba.

MARTÍN KOPPEL: You said you had no health insurance. How did that affect you?

---

1. Under the Cuban Adjustment Act of 1966, the US government allows Cubans to obtain permanent residency one year after their arrival—a fast track to US citizenship not available to immigrants from any other country.

SALANUEVA: After a year or so, I was pregnant with Ivette. As we had no insurance, we had to pay cash up front for all the doctor's visits.

I remembered my first pregnancy in Cuba, where under the maternity law I had the right to paid maternity leave for one year.

I began to have some health problems that often occur with pregnancy—constipation and other symptoms. The doctors paid no attention. It was normal, they told me: I should drink juice. Seven and a half months into the pregnancy, I wound up with hemorrhoids in which blood clots had formed and circulation was blocked. It was extremely painful.

René went with me to the Kendall hospital. I got the kind of treatment you often receive in the US when you go to an emergency room but don't have insurance. There I was with my big belly. And in such pain that I couldn't even sit.

As soon as we walked in the door they called René over: "Your credit card, please." They took $300 and told us to have a seat. But I couldn't sit. I paced, waiting for two and a half hours. If there had been others in the waiting room I would have understood. But there was no one. Then they sent me to gastroenterology. Once again it was, "Show me your Social Security card." "What's your income?" "What are your expenses?" I was moaning in pain, while they were drawing up the bills.

Finally I was seen by a nurse, not a doctor. He gave me an ointment and some tranquilizers. I went home, furious, desperate.

Then René remembered he had given flying lessons to a proctologist who owned a clinic. They had become friends. When René called him, the doctor said what they had done to me was criminal. The clots needed to be cut out right away. When René told him we didn't have insurance, he said, "Bring her here."

The clinic had already closed, but he said, "I'll try to do something." I lay on a stretcher as he operated on me.

I will never forget that experience. People say there are good hospitals in the United States, and it's true, they have tremendous technology. But if you don't have money, you don't have access to it.

Medical personnel try to help you. But most hospitals are businesses. They are supposed to generate profits, and the health care workers are employees. They will get fired if they break the rules. It's the whole system that's a problem.

When Ivette was born

The same thing happened when Ivette was born, in April 1998. René was away at the time, taking a course in Texas. I had just dropped him off at the airport when the labor pains started.

I went to the hospital accompanied by a friend from work. Once again it was the same ordeal: "Take a seat." "Give me all your information." After a while they examined me and said, "You're not ready to give birth yet. Go home." So I went back home, where I was alone with Irmita, who was fourteen. I remember spending the entire night in labor.

The next morning, with my friend, we returned to the hospital. I gave birth around 10:30 p.m. that night. I was alone practically the entire time, with monitors attached all over me. The doctor was taking care of three deliveries at once. A nurse would come to see me once an hour, examine me without a word, then leave. It was my co-workers who came to be with me, young immigrants from the Dominican Republic and Cuba. They practically delivered me.

I was thirty-eight years old. I had high blood pressure. I was in labor for more than twenty-four hours. When Ivette was finally born the umbilical cord was wrapped twice around her neck. I had all the indications that an emergency caesarian section was required. But they left me there until I gave birth. It was a pure miracle we came through it.

Ivette was placed in intensive care as soon as she was born because she had oxygen deprivation. I was put in the postnatal ward, alone. They gave me a bedpan and had me with an IV in one arm and a blood-pressure monitor on the other. I was like that for hours, unable to move. Finally a nurse came and helped me get up to go to the bathroom and bathe.

Contrast with Cuba

This was in Jackson Memorial Hospital. It's the only public hospital in Miami-Dade County, but it has many resources and is very well equipped. I thought: Wow, if we were in Cuba and had all this equipment, the things we could do, with our doctors and the training they have! And that includes the way doctors, nurses, and other health care workers are trained to care for you as a human being. That's why the US government doesn't want Cuba to advance, that's why they've blockaded us.

I felt much better here in Cuba, where I gave birth to Irmita in the Ramón González Coro Maternity Hospital in Havana. It's a small hospital, with the equipment we can afford, but with incredible professional standards and ethical attitudes. I remember giving birth surrounded by so much love, everyone helping me.

SEIU LOCAL 1991

Workers at Miami's Jackson Memorial Hospital protest layoffs and cutbacks they say will affect patient care, April 20, 2011. US hospitals "have tremendous technology. But if you don't have money, you don't have access to it," said Salanueva, describing her experience in US.

RÓGER CALERO: What happened after Ivette was born?

SALANUEVA: Since she was born in the US, Ivette was eligible for Medicaid, and I took her to the clinic every month. When she was a little more than three months old, the doctors told us she had a heart murmur, that it could be serious. That it would have to be followed closely. Each time I took her for a checkup they said she needed a cardiac sonogram. Then, a few months later, they told me Ivette would need heart surgery; they would recommend a specialist.

I was stunned. What a situation! By then René had been arrested. I had lost the house because I couldn't pay the mortgage, and was living in a small apartment. I didn't have a cent. The doctors told me not to worry, that the operation would be covered by Medicaid.

René's grandmother Teté had begun taking care of Ivette after René was arrested. She was a US citizen and lived in Sarasota, four hours northwest of Miami. Teté said, "Look, there's a good children's hospital here and I'm going to take Ivette to be checked by a doctor there."

That cardiologist turned out to be a very fine person. He adored Ivette, and they did all kinds of tests on her. Then one day Teté called me with the news. She'd just heard from the doctor.

He told her, "I'll start with the bad news: I'm not going to be able to see this pretty little girl anymore. The good news is: she's fine. She has no heart problem."

The other doctors had lied. It was a fraud. What they wanted was to pocket the Medicaid money.

I asked myself a thousand times: Can this be true? As someone who grew up in Cuba, so different from capitalist society, I couldn't conceive of such evil.

After I was deported and got Ivette back, the first thing I did was to take her to a cardiologist, because I still had doubts in my mind. The doctors in Havana confirmed there was nothing wrong with her.

Cuba is a country with limited resources that faces a US economic blockade. We may face a shortage of a particular medicine. Doctors may have to substitute one for another, or a patient may remain seriously ill until the medicine arrives.

But the problem is never a lack of medical attention or government indifference. Everything possible is done to ensure people's well-being.

WATERS: What were your other jobs like?

SALANUEVA: By the time René was arrested in

September 1998, I wasn't selling burial plots and cremation services anymore. When Ivette was born four months earlier I had to miss a month of work, and the funeral home fired me. There was no maternity leave at that company.

First I got another telemarketing job selling mortgages. Then a telemarketing job selling English-language learning programs to Spanish-speaking immigrants.

I worked from noon until after 11 p.m., Monday through Friday. We received a basic wage plus a sales commission.

WATERS: You were working from home?
SALANUEVA: I worked at an office during the week. On Saturdays I took work home with me.

The company put inserts promoting the language program in the giveaway Spanish-language newspapers. If you mailed the card back, they sent you a free "dictionary." We called people who returned the cards and explained that they weren't going to learn English with just a dictionary. That they needed a program with teachers and books. That they were very lucky to have contacted this English-language program, blah, blah, blah. And we'd try to sell it to them.

The dictionary was very small, just a pamphlet. When I sent it to René in prison, he told me, "It's the first time in my life I've seen a dictionary in which I know all the words. It's worthless. That's why it's free."

The owners of the company taught you how to sell, how to manipulate potential buyers until they fell for it. They told you what words and tone of voice to use and not to use.

We received a commission after the customer made the first payment. If the customer missed a payment, they'd take back your commission. You had to call the customer and convince them to make a payment or you'd lose your commission.

We had to ask people questions: their name, address, where they were from. We were told that by knowing what country someone was from, you could tell if you were likely to sell to them or not.

Learned about workers' lives

I ended up learning a lot about people's lives. For example, I learned how immigrants from Central America and Mexico had crossed the border. How they lived together crowded into small apartments in the city. What their dreams were, their problems, why they had immigrated—it was always to help their families, to send a little money back home.

The complete program included audiotapes, videos, and a tape recorder. The audiotapes were the least expensive. When I'd hear the things people told me about their situation, I'd say, "Look, buy just the audiotapes—you really won't have time to watch the videos."

I told myself: If they catch me saying this, they're going to fire me! But it was criminal to convince people who earn minimum wage to buy this program. It was worthless—no one learned English with it.

I hated the telemarketing

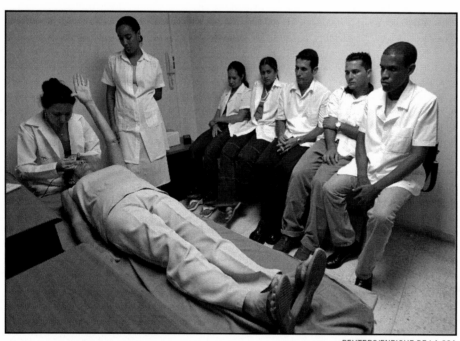

REUTERS/ENRIQUE DE LA OSA

Patient from abroad receives eye treatment at hospital in Havana as medical students observe, September 2006. Cuban program "Operation Miracle" has restored eyesight to well over one million Latin Americans, free of charge. Despite limited resources, health care workers in Cuba "are trained to care for you as a human being," Salanueva said.

jobs. That whole experience is why, to this day, I dislike telephones and don't like to call people.

Many of the people we called were agricultural workers. I'll never forget one of the responses. Among the questions I had to ask was, "Do you work? What's your position?"

And this woman answered, "What's my position? *Agachada*." Bent over. She picked strawberries, stooped over all day. That's what she thought I was asking!

Sometimes we asked, "Have you attended school?" I remember the answers were usually: "No, but I did study a little." "My brothers never got the chance, but I did." "I got to third grade." And so on.

I learned that American businessmen go to Mexico and recruit laborers for six-month contracts to work in agriculture. They are put in a camp they can't leave. Sometimes they aren't paid in cash but in tokens that they have to use in the store owned by the boss. This is something I remember from the history of the sugar mills in Cuba before the revolution. But in this day and age!

I asked one of them, "How did you find out about the English program?"

He said, "The bosses took me to the market one day, and I happened to see an ad in a newspaper. I need to learn English." He asked, "What do you think I should do?"

I couldn't help it. I said what I really thought. "If you want my advice, leave that place—escape. It's better to be undocumented than a slave."

Some undocumented workers had false papers, of course. We would say we just wanted to sell them a language program, and they could use whatever Social Security number they had to establish a credit account. That was one of the hooks—buying the program would help them establish a credit history.

When René and the others were arrested, the US government made a big issue about some of them having false identification documents. They added several years to their prison sentences for having false documents.[2]

_____

2. On top of various "conspiracy" and other charges against the five Cuban revolutionaries, the three who are not US citizens—Gerardo Hernández, Ramón Labañino, and Fernando González—were charged with having false ID documents. Conviction on those counts added five or more years to their sentences.

But there are millions of people in the US with false ID. They *need* undocumented Latinos to work in the US. They do hard physical labor, working long hours at very low wages. And when, like now, they don't need so many due to the economic situation, they just deport people on this or that pretext.

Arrested by 'la migra'

WATERS: What happened after René was arrested?

SALANUEVA: René was taken to the Miami Federal Detention Center, where they kept him in the "hole"—in a punishment cell—for seventeen months. Four months of that was in solitary confinement.

For months he was not allowed to see the two girls. Other inmates in the hole would be taken down to the visiting room when their children came to see them. But not René. They allowed the first visit only after nine months, when Ivette was already thirteen months old.

In February 2000 they moved René out of the hole, and then I was able to visit him once a week for an hour.

All that came to an end August 13 of that year. On that visit—it was René's birthday—he told me about a letter the district attorney had asked him to sign. If he entered a guilty plea and agreed to testify for the prosecution, he wouldn't go to trial and would get a shorter sentence. The letter reminded him that I had permanent resident status and that they could revoke it. René refused to sign, of course.

Three days later, on August 16, I was arrested. They did it to put pressure on him before the trial.

Two agents from the Immigration and Naturalization Service and one from the FBI came to the house. They confiscated my green card and took me to immigration, where they took my fingerprints and photographs. Then they put me in a car to take me to jail.

CALERO: Were you in handcuffs?

SALANUEVA: Oh yes. A policewoman escorted me in the car. Her job was to play soft cop. She knew the hard times I'd gone through the past two years, she said. "A woman living alone, who

Planting celery in Clewiston, Florida, January 2007. Salanueva learned about conditions of immigrants and other fellow workers during her four years in US. She was deported in 2000 after her husband, René González, refused to testify against his four comrades in frame-up trial.

René hugged me and said, "You look good in orange."

When I told him I had been arrested by immigration agents, he said, "That means they will probably deport you to carry out the threat in the letter they handed me. We must be prepared for that."

WATERS: How long were you in the Fort Lauderdale prison?

SALANUEVA: Three months. It's a state prison, but they rent two cells to the federal government to hold immigrants and people on their way to federal court. They use it as a punishment facility for inmates from Krome, the immigration detention center in Miami.

My cell had no windows. The lights were on twenty-four hours a day, and a camera was taping you. The cell had four cots, a table, a toilet, a wash basin, and a shower with a curtain.

I shared the cell with Cuban women, a woman from Colombia, and women from Haiti, with whom I got along very well.

During these three months, René and I wrote to each other. I received his letters from prison. But none of my letters were delivered to him.

CALERO: What about the response of your co-workers? Didn't one of them help you and René communicate with each other while you were in jail?

SALANUEVA: Yes, that was Marina. She was from Peru, a hard worker. We respected each other. She was very religious; she knew I wasn't a believer. When I was arrested she visited me in jail. She told me to be calm and gave me a Bible, with a beautiful dedication, which I still have.

On one visit she asked if I had spoken with René. I explained that you're not allowed to make calls from one prison to another.

Now, at the telemarketing company they gave us tape recorders to use during sales calls. We

just had a baby and has an older child. Has it been difficult for you?" Imagine! Of course, they knew everything.

Then the policewoman said, "You know, these things can be worked out, the charges can be reduced. But your husband hasn't been willing to cooperate."

She asked if I wanted to see René. I knew they were trying to manipulate me. But, I thought, this is my chance. "Yes, I want to see him," I said.

First they took me to the state prison in Fort Lauderdale, thirty miles up the coast. There they put me in a filthy, stained prison uniform and locked me in a cell. Fifteen minutes later they took me out of the cell, put me in a car, and took me back down to Miami, to the Federal Detention Center where René was. They just wanted me to see what it was going to be like in jail.

They dressed me in that orange prison uniform to try to shake up René. They brought him into a room and sat us down facing each other, with all the FBI agents there. When I saw him I was overcome by emotion, because I felt it was going to be the last time I'd see him for a long time. It turned out to be true.

would ask the customer to say his name, give us some information, and state that he agreed to the terms of the contract.

Marina said, "Remember, I have a recorder at home. Let's have René call me. I'll accept the call and record René's message for you. Then you call me, I'll record you, and when René calls me again I'll play the recorder so he can hear your message. When you call again, you'll be able to listen to René's message."

Deported to Cuba

It turned out to be farewell messages to each other, because by then I was about to be deported.

They deported me on November 22, 2000, just five days before the trial of the five began.

WATERS: On what basis did the US government deport you?

SALANUEVA: In immigration court, no evidence was presented that implicated me in anything. The prosecutors said I knew about my husband's activity. The judge asked them to show proof that I belonged to this group of spies that had been arrested or that I knew what they were doing.

"The trial hasn't started yet," the prosecutor said. "I can only say she's part of the group, and her daughters are too."

The judge asked, "The daughters? How old are they?"

"Yes, yes, the daughters. One is fourteen years old and the other is two."

"But how can you say the daughters knew?"

"OK, not now, but in the future they could know," said the prosecutor.

It was hysterical. From that time on, we called Ivette the "baby spy."

The judge said, "Well, although I see no evidence, I have the authority, on the basis of suspicion, to revoke her residency and deport her." And that's what he did.

After the deportation hearing I asked to see René. They said no. Irmita was already in Cuba; she had come here on vacation before my arrest. I asked immigration to bring Ivette to the airport, so I could take her to Cuba with me. They said no, Ivette was a US citizen, and she was not subject to deportation.

"And how is she going to stay in the US if I am going to be deported and René is in prison?" I asked.

They replied that we would have to find a relative to travel with Ivette and give that relative a power of attorney. As it happened, René's mother, Irma [Sehwerert], had been granted a visa to visit René. So Ivette returned to Cuba with Irma the day after I was deported.

'Many in Cuba need to hear this'

KOPPEL: I understand that Irmita got support from some of her friends at school.

SALANUEVA: Yes, that was at the end of the trial. Irmita was back living in Cuba by then, and she traveled to Miami to attend the sentencing in December 2001.

Irmita's friends saw her in the newspapers and on television. Some of them defied all the hostile propaganda and went to the courtroom to support her.

I was in the United States for four years. In that brief time I learned what it meant to live and work in that country as just one more worker. These were my experiences, but there are millions of similar stories by immigrants in the United States.

In Cuba many people need to hear these things, both those of my generation—I was born in 1959—and today's youth. These are things that in Cuba you only read about in books or hear from your grandparents. You might think it's part of the past. That today capitalism isn't like that. But practical experiences like the ones I went through teach you more about life under capitalism than anything you can read. They show you why a revolution was necessary in Cuba.

Having gone through these experiences, I value even more all that we've achieved in our country. Everything we cannot allow them to take away from us. The gains we can never give up. That's what the five are defending; it's why they keep them in jail. And it's why we will never stop fighting to free them.

JULY 16 AND 23, 2012

PART III

Who Are the Cuban Five?

Touring art exhibits broaden support for fight to free the Cuban Five

Above: Several paintings by Antonio Guerrero and cartoons by Gerardo Hernández (examples on left and right, respectively) were part of *Beyond the Frame* art exhibit in United Kingdom, April–May 2012. The exhibit featured works by 46 Cuban and other artists, most donated to raise funds for Cuban Five defense campaign. **Right:** Hundreds viewed display at London gallery before it traveled to Glasgow, Scotland.

JULIE KING

LINDA HARRIS/MILITANT

Left: Some 150 people attended launch of exhibit of cartoons by Gerardo Hernández at art gallery in Sydney, Australia, April 19, 2012.

'TWELVE MEN AND TWO CATS'
With Gerardo Hernández and His Platoon in Angola

By Mary-Alice Waters

When Gerardo Hernández Nordelo graduated from Cuba's Institute for Advanced Study of International Relations (ISRI) in 1989, like hundreds of thousands of other Cubans had done, he volunteered for duty in Angola. The Revolutionary Armed Forces (FAR) of Cuba was then engaged in the final stages of a nearly sixteen-year internationalist mission, fighting alongside the People's Armed Forces for the Liberation of Angola (FAPLA), to defend the government of that former Portuguese colony against the invading forces of the apartheid regime of South Africa and its imperialist-backed allies based in Zaire.

In 1989–90, Lieutenant Hernández led the Cuban-Angolan Scouting Platoon of twelve men attached to the Eleventh Tactical Group of the Tenth Tank Brigade, stationed in the Angolan province of Cabinda.

The following account of those years is by José Luis Palacio, a mechanic by trade and one of the men who served under Hernández in Cabinda. It was originally published under the title "Twelve Men and Two Cats" in March 2006 in *Guerrillero*, the provincial newspaper of Pinar del Río in western Cuba.

Palacio's tribute to the leadership qualities of Hernández—or simply "Gerardo" as he is known to millions around the world fighting for his freedom—goes far to explain why the US government has singled him out for the brutal and vindictive treatment reported in the accompanying story. Among the Cuban Five, Hernández was given the most draconian penalty of all—two life sentences plus fifteen years. He has been denied the right to receive visits from his wife, Adriana Pérez, since his 1998 arrest.

Hernández sent a photocopy of the *Guerrillero* article to me as one of the editors of *Malcolm X,*

Black Liberation, and the Road to Workers Power by Jack Barnes, published by Pathfinder Press. That book, which Hernández had received earlier this year, includes one of the photos on these pages— the picture of Hernández together with other members of his platoon around a cooking fire. The other two photos of the platoon printed here were mailed by Gerardo from the maximum-security penitentiary in Victorville, California, where he is being held.

In accompanying letters, Hernández commented:

> It's been twenty years, but I remember as if it were today the moment when we took that photo around the fire in Angola. We were making a *dulce de coco* [a coconut dessert]. I remember everyone's names, including the two Angolan combatants in the picture, who were part of our scouting team.
>
> Several Cuban combatants from my platoon often write to me, including three members of what they called my "Matancera squad," since all of them were from Matanzas—José Ramón Zamora, Fidel Martell, and Wilfredo Pérez Corcho. All three are peasants, very modest people, and very revolutionary. They sent me these two photos, which I am now sharing with you.
>
> The quality of the originals is not very good due to the passage of time and the conditions under which they were developed and printed. . . .
>
> In the photo with the tank . . . standing on the ground is José Luis Palacio, from Pinar del Río. For some years I have kept an interview that Palacio gave to the newspaper in his province, which moved me very much when

I read it. I'll look for it among my papers and send you a copy.

I have great admiration for all those compañeros who volunteered for such a mission. At that time they were practically youngsters. I had been asked to give them classes in certain subjects, that is, I was supposed to teach them, but I was the one who wound up learning a lot from them. Angola was a great school for everyone.

The identifications in the captions were provided by Hernández. The comments in brackets in the interview below are his also.

Translation from the original Spanish is by the *Militant*.

❧

By Zenia Regalado

A Pinar del Río native was in Angola with Lieutenant Gerardo Hernández Nordelo. He remembers him as lively and jocular, always drawing cartoons of the soldiers in his reconnaissance platoon; reading Che's diary. The first to get up in the morning and the last to go to bed. Always very concerned with the health of the men under his command.

When a group of twelve men have to sleep two and a half meters underground, shake off the homesickness that slowly eats at them with each delayed letter, march through snake-infested terrain, that's when friendship soars to its greatest heights.

So one can understand why José Luis Palacio Cuní would feel out of sorts when he returned from Angola in 1991 and why he would miss the down-to-earth camaraderie and kidding around by those platoon mates of the Tenth Tank Brigade in Cabinda.

At night they killed time playing seven-piece dominoes or playing cards. The latter was the favorite entertainment of Lieutenant Gerardo Hernández Nordelo, [*Actually it was dominoes.—GH*] who was good-humored and always roused them at 5:00 a.m. with that characteristic expression of his: "Stand up, soldiers! As straight as Cuba's palm trees!"

At that time nobody imagined that Gerardo—who shared the same hole with them—would become a hero, and that he would have to withstand even greater tests—nothing less than imprisonment in the United States.

None of Palacio's friends wanted to believe him that afternoon when they were watching television and, in the middle of a little party, this dark-skinned man who lives in the new twelve-story building at "Hermanos Cruz" told them, "Damn! That man in the photo was my leader in Angola. It's Lieutenant Nordelo!"

Two cats in the platoon

Palacio was in Angola, in Cabinda, for two years and three months. He had been working at the Machinery and Equipment Repair Enterprise, what was then the EREA, when he was called to fulfill his duty as a reservist. It was 1989, and he left behind a daughter who was just a

Gerardo Hernández with members of scouting platoon in Cabinda, Angola, 1989–90. Atop tank, from left: Pembele, Angolan combatant; Adolfo, center front; Henry, center back; Hernández. Standing in front: José Luis Palacio, interviewed in this article.

little over three years old.

How did you all adjust to sleeping in the dugout? was one of the first questions we asked in our interview.

"The dugouts were six meters long and two or three meters wide. It wasn't easy getting used to sleeping there, but when you know it's safer than having your body out in the open, you have to do it.

"I was the only Pinar del Río native among those twelve men. The majority were from Matanzas, and we also had some *orientales* [from eastern Cuba] and some from Havana. At night when we were down there, someone would start telling the others that the most beautiful place in Cuba was Viñales; then someone else would jump in talking about his province, and so on. . . .

"A young guy from Matanzas, as soon as he arrived, began to take care of two cats. Those little animals really were internationalist soldiers too, because there were mice underground, and while we slept we often heard the cats hunting. They were very attached to us.

"Our lieutenant completed his mission, and then Gerardo arrived, a graduate of the Institute for Advanced Study of International Relations. The head of the Eleventh Tactical Group told us, 'This is your new commander.' I remember very well Nordelo's first words:

" 'I'm going to share the happiness, the sadness, and all other emotions with you. I'll just be one of

Hernández with Cuban and Angolan combatants in Angola making dulce de coco (a coconut dessert). "First row, from left to right: Aldolfo, Pembele (Angolan), Nelson Abreu, and Gabriel Basquito (Angolan). Behind them are Yoel and myself."—GH

you, like a brother, simply another human being.' We liked him a lot from the start.

"At night he would talk about when he was at the university, about his life as a student, about his cartoons, about his mother and his wife.

"He was very funny and knew how to tell jokes. In class he would give us a six-minute break, and during that time he would draw cartoons of us and say, 'That's what you were like in class.'

"When he saw someone was sad, Gerardo would even show him his own letters. When you're so far away, nothing is worth more than someone writing you.

"We played baseball in our free time. Was he good? To tell the truth, no, he wasn't. He was a pitcher, and since we were playing for fun, it didn't matter much. . . .

"He set up a radio; he always had to be doing something. He wrote the communiqués and jokes that were read by a soldier."

El Corcho

The tall, slender, dark-skinned man recalled that in the platoon there was a very thin young man named Pérez Corcho, who they nicknamed "El Corcho" [The Cork].

"Everyone would call to him, 'El Corcho, come here' and 'El Corcho, go there.' When his birthday came along, Gerardo got the idea that we should celebrate it. He asked for permission, and it was granted.

"For the occasion we made wine from rice and from pineapples, which were very abundant in the area. That day we didn't go to the unit's main mess hall." [*It wasn't wine but a kind of fruit drink, because alcohol was prohibited. —GH*]

Many of those in the group of twelve had no idea how to cook, but they invented things. Gerardo wrote some jokes for the occasion and a communiqué. He always combined happy themes with patriotic ones, says his former subordinate.

And did you have a strategy for dealing with the snakes?

"There were lots of cobras there. We had orders to sleep with mosquito netting and to put one boot inside the other so as not to leave them a space they could slide into, since they always seek body warmth.

"Gerardo would be the last to go to bed and always told us, 'Stuff your boots together the way you now know how to.' He always paid attention to those details, even though he was very young.

"Every third or fourth day we marched forty or fifty kilometers [twenty-five or thirty miles] through the jungle on our reconnaissance missions. We went together in a platoon made up of Angolans from FAPLA and the Cubans.

"Once one of the Angolans discovered a six-meter-long boa and killed it. They had a lot of respect for boas and said that we Cubans didn't fear even those beasts, since we didn't kill them.

"Lieutenant Nordelo always alerted us to everything, and one of the things he stressed most was the need to respect our own families and the families that lived there.

"I had previously seen on television Angola's poverty and what the UNITA troops[1] were doing, but none of that could compare with what I saw afterward. Children living in very bad conditions, living in those huts, skinny, emaciated, and I couldn't help comparing them to ours and thinking that sometimes we weren't really conscious of what we had.

"For me, Angola was a school. I learned to value life and internationalism more, and to give a little of myself.

"One of Gerardo's many good ideas was about the children of the place where we were. He asked people to make homemade toys for the children, even rag dolls. It was very nice."

When you saw Gerardo on TV, what did you feel?

"At first I was very sad, thinking of a man who

---

1. Originally founded to fight Portuguese colonial rule, the National Union for the Total Independence of Angola (UNITA), led by Jonas Savimbi, allied itself in 1975 with the racist apartheid regime in South Africa and US imperialism in an effort to overthrow the newly independent Angolan government. Some 375,000 Cuban combatants fought in Angola alongside FAPLA against pro-imperialist forces, including UNITA. Cuba ended its internationalist combat mission there in 1991 after the South African military was defeated and forced to withdraw from Angola and grant independence to nearby Namibia.

Cuban Angolan platoon under command of Gerardo Hernández

Platoon attached to Eleventh Tactical Group, Tenth Tank Brigade, Cabinda, Angola, under command of Lieutenant Gerardo Hernández Nordelo, 1989–90. Starting with front row from left to right, Hernández wrote, are: "Wilfredo Pérez Corcho (with a cat), Fidel Martell (with the other cat), Palacio, Bouza, and Adolfo. (Bouza is from the Zapata Swamp area, and the last that I heard of him, he was an official of the municipal Cuban Communist Party in Soplillar.) I'm in the middle, and behind are Gabriel Basquito (Angolan), Henry, Manuel (who also graduated from the ISRI [Institute for Advanced Study of International Relations] and may now be a diplomat), José Ramón Zamora, two compañeros whose names unfortunately I cannot remember now, Nelson Abreu, another compañero (with the sunglasses) whose name I cannot recall, and Carlos Amores, with the camera, our current ambassador to Malaysia. For most of those whose names I cannot recall, it's because they were in the platoon for only a short time after I arrived because they completed their missions and returned to Cuba."

was such a revolutionary, such a good comrade, who had been so concerned for all of us, and who was today imprisoned—in the United States.

"But now I see it differently. It makes me happy to remember that the lieutenant at whose side I spent so much time is today a symbol of patriotism, that he has not given in. He has withstood so much; they haven't even allowed him to see his wife. That man, who was taking care of all of us, has not been able to have children!

"At the same time, I feel more revolutionary and committed. I also hope he will return and that those twelve Cubans will be able to meet again to recall the times we lived through in Angola."

Palacio, a modest man, a party member, a refrigeration and air conditioning mechanic in a cold storage plant, has not written Gerardo because he didn't have the address of the prison. Nor does he seek the limelight in recounting his days together with that lieutenant who liked to read so much.

It was Palacio's friend Félix Peña, an official of the provincial committee of the party, who encouraged him to speak with a reporter—to share with many more people his experiences with that genuine Cuban, whose ideals support him as straight as the Cuban palms he talked about to his men, as if to remind them they were born in a small island accustomed to nobleness.

Hernández's scouting platoon was part of a tactical group belonging to the Tenth Tank Brigade in Cabinda, which took part in reconnaissance missions to protect Cuban units and troops.

When he gave classes to his soldiers, Palacio reports, Gerardo would stress to them the importance of sharpening their skills for observing the enemy in order to track them.

A scout looks for signs on the ground indicating where the adversary might be. He must study the makeup of the opposing army, its weaponry.

All members of that twelve-man platoon—a symbolic number in the history of Cuba—have a photo of the group. Gerardo himself took it. In different ways this patriot has things in common with Ignacio Agramonte,[2] that fierce attorney, that man of letters and also of action in the fields of Cuba, capable of wielding a machete but also of writing tender lines to his wife.

And this Cuban hero, who has grown while locked up in a US prison cell, left for his wife Adriana, along with the song *Dulce abismo* [Sweet abyss] by Silvio Rodríguez, this poem by Roberto Fernández Retamar entitled *"Filin"*:[3]

> *If they tell me you have gone away*
> *And will not come back*
> *I won't believe it*
> *I will wait for you and wait for you.*
>
> *If they tell you I have gone*
> *And will not return*
> *Don't believe it*
> *Wait for me*
> *Always.*

AUGUST 16, 2010

2. Ignacio Agramonte (1841–73) was one of the most outstanding political and military leaders of Cuba's first independence war against Spain. Division commander of the Liberation Army in Camagüey Province. He rose to the rank of major general. He was killed in battle.

3. *Filin* (feeling) was a genre of popular Cuban music that developed in Havana during a period of growing social unrest in the 1940s and '50s, incorporating elements of both jazz and Cuban bolero.

RAMÓN LABAÑINO: 'FOR A WORLD FREE OF THE DEATH PENALTY AND BARBARISM'

By Martín Koppel

Ramón Labañino, writing on behalf of the Cuban Five, sent a message (see box) to family members and supporters of Troy Davis on September 23, 2011. Two days earlier the state of Georgia had executed Davis, an African American framed for the 1989 killing of a policeman in Savannah, Georgia.

No physical evidence linked Davis to the killing. Seven of the nine non-police witnesses against him at the trial subsequently recanted or changed their testimony, several saying that the police pressured

them to falsely name Davis as the killer.

A broad international campaign fought the execution, and Davis won several stays of execution. Nonetheless, the Georgia and US Supreme Courts refused to grant a new trial and President Barack Obama declined to commute the sentence.

Davis maintained his innocence to the end. The day before he was put to death, he released a statement saying, "The struggle for justice doesn't end with me. This struggle is for all the Troy Davises who came before me and all the ones who will

Brothers and sisters:

We feel deeply the horrific execution of Troy Davis. It is another terrible injustice and stain on the history of this country. We join in the pain felt by his relatives, friends and brothers across the world. Now we have another cause, another flag, to pursue our struggle for a better world for all, free of the death penalty and barbarism.

In Troy's honor, and all the innocents of the world, we must continue, united, until the final victory!

Our most heart-felt condolences!
Five fraternal embraces,

Antonio Guerrero
Fernando González
Gerardo Hernández
René González
Ramón Labañino

Left: Troy Davis.
Below: Demonstrators in Atlanta call for halt to execution of Troy Davis, September 16, 2011. Davis, framed up for 1989 killing of a policeman, was executed five days after this protest.

MACEO DIXON/MILITANT

come after me." His final message was, "I ask my friends and family to continue to fight this fight."

'Soldier of silence'

Labañino graduated in economics from the University of Havana, where he also distinguished himself in the university's five-year military training program. He became an officer of Cuba's Ministry of Interior.

In a January 2012 interview Labañino said his mother had always wanted him to wear a Cuban military uniform. "Of course, I could never tell my mother that from an early age I was also fulfilling her dreams too," he said. "I was a soldier of silence, without the regular uniform. I was one of those who, out of the necessities imposed by important missions, must conceal their real identity in order to carry out work on behalf of our country."

When in 1992 he accepted an assignment from the Cuban intelligence service to work undercover in the United States, he could not tell his family. His wife, Elizabeth Palmeiro, thought he was in Spain working for a business. "I didn't know he was part of that anonymous army of Cubans who leave everything—their family, their jobs—to work for their country, trying to prevent terrorist, violent actions against Cuba," she said.

In a 2005 interview with the Cuban magazine *Bohemia,* she explained that during those six long years, months would go by with no word from him. And unlike other Cubans working abroad during the difficult economic crisis in the 1990s, he never sent any money home to help out. Some of her friends, she said, kept urging her to dump him as a worthless deadbeat.

Despite these uncertainties, Palmeiro told the magazine, she never stopped trusting that "down-to-earth, modest man" who during the worst of the Special Period never complained about the blackouts, the limited food on the table, or having

to ride his bike to go anywhere in the city.

One day, she said, after a long stretch of not hearing from him, Ramón came home, and in a few words told her enough to dispel her doubts. Palmeiro quickly understood the conditions and hazards under which he was operating and why. "I'm not the only one—I'm neither the first nor the last. And you, too, are not the only woman who faces something like this," Labañino told her. "The rest I leave to your intelligence and understanding."

Palmeiro said that for her, "that was sufficient."

After Labañino's arrest in September 1998, "twenty-seven months went by with no communication between us," she said. "Since he didn't reveal his true identity until the beginning of the trial, he couldn't make calls to Cuba."

In that trial, Labañino was convicted of "conspiracy to gather and transmit to a foreign government information relating to national defense" and other trumped-up charges. He was sentenced to life in prison plus eighteen years. In 2009, that sentence was reduced to thirty years after an appeals court ruled it exceeded federal guidelines (see article on page 63). Labañino is currently being held at the medium-security prison in Jesup, Georgia.

At his December 2001 sentencing hearing, Labañino told the courtroom that in face of decades of US-backed attacks by counterrevolutionary forces, "Cuba has the basic right to defend itself. That is all that we have done, [and] as long as this criminal policy against my people persists, there will continue to be men like us."

"Whether you like it or not," he said, "Cuba is an independent and sovereign country. It has its own legitimate government, its own president, its own martyrs and heroes, and its own convictions. . . .

"I will wear the prison uniform with the same honor and pride with which a soldier wears his most prized insignia!"

OCTOBER 10, 2011

POET AND PAINTER: LEARNING TO DRAW IN PRISON

By Antonio Guerrero

In the article below, Antonio Guerrero tells the story of how he learned to draw and paint in prison.

Convicted of conspiracy to gather and transmit information relating to national defense and other trumped-up charges, Guerrero was sentenced in 2001 to life in prison plus ten years. In October 2009 his sentence was reduced to twenty-one years and ten months, after an appeals court ruled that the sentences against three of the Cuban Five—Guerrero, Ramón Labañino, and Fernando González—exceeded federal sentencing guidelines (see article on resentencing hearing on page 62).

When he wrote this account in 2007, Guerrero was locked up at the US Penitentiary in Florence, Colorado. In January 2012 he was transferred to the medium-security Federal Correctional Institution in Marianna, Florida.

Guerrero is also a poet. A volume of his prison poems has been published in English and Spanish under the title *From My Altitude.* An exhibit of his paintings and drawings with the same title is touring cities in the United States and other countries. There have been shows in Washington state, Oregon, California, Colorado, Texas, Kentucky, Minnesota, Michigan, Maine, New York, and Washington, D.C., as well as in London and in Glasgow, Scotland.

The translation into English is by the *Militant*.

November 15, 2007—At the beginning of 2003, when I had just completed my first year of imprisonment in this penitentiary in Florence, Colorado, I searched, anxiously, for something that would occupy my time, far from the tense and violent atmosphere that reigned in this prison.

Poetry had been an effective weapon to overcome the long periods of unjust punishment in the cells of the so-called "hole," as well as the prolonged "lockdowns," which the whole prison population here was subjected to after any violent incident. But with the constant commotion during the "normal" routine of the prison, my muse, sometimes startled, would fade away and fail to inspire me.

So, one fine day, I went to the so-called "Hobby Craft," (Department of Recreation) and I found a prisoner giving pencil drawing classes; basically everyone was making a portrait. I was impressed above all by the work of the instructor and I asked him how I could participate in his class. It turned out this person was very enthusiastic about teaching what he knew, and even more fortunate, he was in my dorm unit.

He gave me some materials and by the following day I had decided on my first project: a portrait of my beloved mother.

Before I even finished this first work, that sudden and vile punishment came in which we were isolated in cells in the "hole," the five of us in our five prisons. It was the result of the application of the Special Administrative Measures (SAM), ordered by the US Attorney General. International solidarity and the energetic demands of our attorneys made it possible for that unjust punishment to be lifted in one month.

It so happened that upon returning to my dormitory unit I had "lost" my placement and they had no cell in which to put me. I noticed that the inmate who gave the drawing classes was alone in his cell, and I told the guard: Put me with him. He was surprised because that prisoner was Black, what they call here Afro-American, and here it is rarely seen (nor is it accepted by the prisoners) that prisoners of different races or groups (or gangs) live together.

As I hoped, Andre accepted me into his cell. Living together my interest in drawing grew and we formed a good friendship.

Every day I dedicated several hours to drawing. My first five works required the help of the instructor. But I remember we were locked down for almost a month, and Andre told me, "Now you are going to do portraits on your own." And it was during that lockdown that I made the portraits of José Martí and Cintio Vitier on my own. When I finished I realized that I could now continue my independent course, and it was the right moment because Andre was transferred to another penitentiary in California as soon as that lockdown was lifted.

A Native Indian, also imprisoned in my unit, took Andre's place as instructor. We also became good friends. Every night we worked together on different projects. The combination of Andre's and the new instructor's teachings allowed me to create my own method of work.

On some occasions I was able to finish a painting in one day. Up to now I have created more than 100 works with pencil.

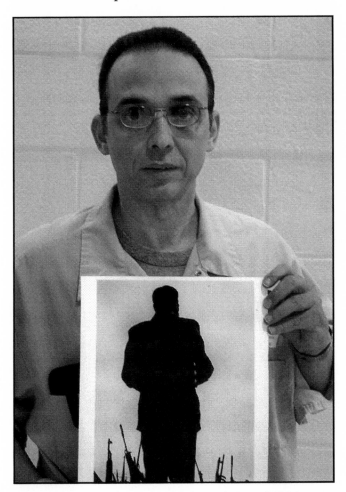

Antonio Guerrero in prison with his painting of Fidel Castro.

In 2005 I met a prisoner who offered to teach me calligraphy. I was interested in making a clean copy of all the poems I had written in these years of imprisonment. I acquired some essential materials, but I realized that the watercolors that I used as ink were not good, nor was there enough. Looking for something that could take the place of the ink (which they don't authorize for purchase) a bunch of watercolor paint tubes fell into my hands from another prisoner. But using it for the calligraphy proved to be another disaster and I asked myself, "What do I do with all this?" I decided to try them out with small paintings. Nobody here painted with that technique, so I could only count on the help of some books I had bought with the paintings. Little by little I was gaining confidence in my strokes with the handful of brushes that I had and I started setting bigger goals.

Color gave another life to my creations. Painting made me happy. In one or two days now I finished each work.

With the help of a great friend of Cuba and the Five, Cindy O'Hara, who sent me books and photos, I was able to finish two interesting projects in watercolor: the birds that are endemic to Cuba and the species of guacamayos. Other caring friends in the United States, like the tireless Priscilla Felia, have sent me books that have been very useful for my self-taught progress in these and other techniques.

At the end of 2005 a prisoner arrived from Marion in Illinois, who began to show impressive pastel photo works. They placed him in my dormitory unit and right away I became interested in this new technique. I acquired some materials, following his instructions. He had a great will to teach, but soon he had problems and was taken to the "hole." He never returned to the general population.

Once again I found myself wondering what to do with the painting materials I had acquired and once more I returned to the books to immerse myself in an unfamiliar technique. I decided a portrait of Che would be my first work in pastel and after that I undertook a project of fourteen portraits of the most relevant figures of our history. I have continued using pastels without interruption in my artwork. The most recent with this technique are a group of nudes, which I have used to study the human figure and the different skin tones under the effect of lights and shadows.

Just two months ago, also being self-taught, I broached painting in acrylics, using an air gun (in English this technique is known as "airbrushing").

And oil painting didn't escape my interest either. Here they only authorize a type of oil paint that is soluble in water and although it is not the traditional paint it is similar enough in its use and results. Up to now I have completed five works with this technique.

Without a specific plan or guide, I believe that it was the right path to first do pencil portraits, and then to take on watercolor, pastels, and finally, oils. Of course, all of these works have been without benefit of the professional instruction that an art school would give, or the guide of an instructor with real knowledge of plastic arts.

What is most important, I think, is that I have overcome imprisonment with a healthy and useful activity like plastic arts. Each work expresses not only my human essence but that of the Five, united by unbreakable principles.

The little I have learned I share unselfishly with other prisoners, and, at times, with great patience. "Truth desires art" as José Martí said, and truth reigns in our hearts, forged with love and commitment to the just cause of our heroic people: That is my motivation for each work of art!

AUGUST 23, 2010

Detail of work by Antonio Guerrero, painted in Florence, Colorado, federal prison.

NATALIE MORRISON/MILITANT

Minneapolis: Students from North High School view exhibit of artwork by Antonio Guerrero at Homewood Studios, in heart of Black community. Guerrero's works have been shown across country.

'IN PRISON I SAW FERNANDO'S SPIRIT OF RESISTANCE'

By Carlos Alberto Torres

The following tribute to Fernando González was given by Carlos Alberto Torres, a longtime Puerto Rican independence fighter and himself a former political prisoner. Torres was speaking at an Oct. 29, 2010, meeting in San Juan, Puerto Rico, organized by the Puerto Rico Committee for Solidarity with Cuba, which called for the release of all the Puerto Rican *independentista* prisoners as well as the Cuban Five.

In March 2012 Torres was in New York campaigning for the release of the three Puerto Rican independence fighters currently locked up in US prisons: Oscar López Rivera, who has already served 31 years; Avelino González Claudio, incarcerated since 2008; and Norberto González Claudio, in prison since 2011.

Speaking with *Militant* reporters during his New York visit, Torres noted that he had shared five of his years at the federal prison in Oxford, Wisconsin, with Fernando González, whom he described as "unbreakable." Torres also met González's mother, Magali Llort, and his wife, Rosa Aurora Freijanes, during their visits to Oxford, and expressed admiration for their "incredible" determination and dignity.

In 2007 González was transferred to the federal prison in Terre Haute, Indiana, where he came to know fellow prisoner Oscar López. He is currently in the minimum-security federal prison in Safford, Arizona.

Torres, 59, was released on parole in July 2010 after serving 30 years of a 78-year sentence in federal prisons for "seditious conspiracy" and other frame-up charges. He was one of the longest-held political prisoners in the world.

Asked by students at Hostos Community College whether he felt he had wasted his life in prison, Torres replied, "No, for me it was simply another place to carry out my political work. I never stopped being part of the struggle. I was able to raise the consciousness of fellow prisoners." He said he did not regret those years "because it was part of my responsibility in the fight for my homeland."

Under parole restrictions Torres is barred from "associating with" anyone previously sentenced on felony charges, including former political prisoners. His travel must be approved by parole authorities. During his New York speaking tour, for example, he was not able to participate in an event with fellow independence fighter Ricardo Jiménez, who was released from prison in 1999 and has served out his parole.

These restrictions, however, have not stopped Torres from speaking wherever he can. Last year he toured several cities in Illinois, California, Oregon, Washington, and Tennessee. Torres, who taught himself painting and ceramics in prison, today works as a ceramic artist in Camuy, Puerto Rico.

The translation is by the *Militant*.

Good evening, *compañeros* and *compañeras*,

In 2002, at the Oxford, Wisconsin, federal prison, as I was painting a work in oil called *Resurrection*, another inmate told me one of the five Cuban political prisoners had arrived. It was Fernando González Llort. Prison officials called him "Rubén Campa," a pseudonym Fernando had used before his arrest.

After getting to know him and a few brief conversations, he told me his name was Fernando, not Rubén. He said, without any sign of annoyance, that the prison officials knew this but hadn't corrected it, perhaps out of bureaucratic indifference.

It seemed to me almost humorous that this Cuban, so reserved and careful, always respectful and correct, showed so little concern at being called the wrong name. I too had used a pseudonym during the years I was underground, and I remembered that after my arrest in 1980, it was actually something of a relief to be able to use my own name again.

Fernando's apparent indifference about what name he was called was a detail that revealed an important aspect of the person his experiences had created. It didn't matter to him what definition prison officials imposed, because that had nothing to do with who he was. He kept a wall between them and him. Even in these circumstances, the only thing that mattered to him was how he defined himself. He and I were in complete agreement on this.

Over time we got to know each other more and understand each other better. I learned something of the arrest of the Cuban Five. Although I wasn't familiar with the details of the charges against them and the sentences the federal court gave to Fernando, Ramón, René, Antonio, and Gerardo, it was easy to imagine the duplicity and injustice behind their imprisonment. I also didn't know, but could imagine, the abuse and isolation the five Cuban patriots had suffered since their arrest.

Before me was an honest, committed man with a deep political consciousness. Despite the hardships he had been through, he showed no bitterness over his situation. He was proud he was carrying out his duty for Cuba, his nation and homeland. I have no doubt that all five Cuban heroes, defenders of the safety of their country and their people, are men of outstanding uprightness and unbreakable commitment. The five have been punished because of the US government's hatred of the Cuban Revolution. Until I met Fernando, I thought this kind of

mistreatment of prisoners was reserved solely for Puerto Rican political prisoners.

Over time we shared many things. Rare was the time that Fernando wouldn't accompany me on walks in the prison yard. They became a time to talk about everything: personal memories, heated debates, banter that sometimes tailed off into jokes or recollections of girlfriends from our youth.

During the years we were both inmates in Wisconsin, I think we got to know each other as two individuals who were fighting for their homeland and were sacrificing themselves for it as well. We reached an understanding, I believe, that the struggles for the independence of our two countries were deeply related. We are still fighting to win Puerto Rico's independence—Cuba is fighting to protect and preserve hers. There is a saying: that Cuba and Puerto Rico are petals from the same flower, sister islands with a long history of shared struggles. There, in prison in Oxford, Wisconsin, the truth of that saying was demonstrated in flesh and blood.

I learned more details about the unjust trial that kept the five Cuban heroes locked up in prison. I got to know better the character and spirit of resistance to injustice shown by Gerardo, Ramón, Antonio, René, and Fernando. And I was able see the determination to fight and the love that marked their families.

I should say something about what the support of family members, friends, and compañeros means when you're in prison. That support is absolutely essential. It sustains us, it gives us strength when we are feeling the weight of imprisonment. The love and commitment of our loved ones helps us put things back in perspective when prison conditions get to us so much that we lose focus. It's not possible to capture in words the full importance of contact and visits with our loved ones.

Our jailers know this too. For prison officials, contact

Supporters of Carlos Alberto Torres (black shirt) welcome him in San Juan, Puerto Rico, July 2010, when he arrives after spending 30 years in US prisons because of his activity in support of Puerto Rico's independence.

and visits with our families can be turned into a weapon to use against us. For the Puerto Rican political prisoners, and later for the five Cuban political prisoners as well, one tactic for attacking us has been to interfere with or deny contact or visits with our loved ones. They harass them or bar their visits. It shouldn't surprise us, then, that both in the case of Oscar and Avelino, and in that of Gerardo, Ramón, René, Antonio, and Fernando, the tactic of interfering with family visits becomes a club to try to beat them down.

Despite the many restrictions and limitations, I had the honor and pleasure of meeting Fernando's mother and wife. They are kind human beings, tireless and dedicated workers. Not only are they doing everything they can to bring Fernando and his compañeros home. They are fighting women who defend their people with a strong sense of commitment and responsibility. Although I haven't met personally the family members of the other

Cuban political prisoners, I know they too are fighting for them and support them, no matter what restrictions the jailers impose. Those same close family ties are something our patriots Oscar and Avelino have shared as well.

Today, both Cuba and Puerto Rico have patriots behind bars in US federal prisons. We have the same enemy, the same jailer. The same zombie—to use a Haitian term—who wants to bury Oscar and Avelino alive in the depths of the prison is trying to bury Fernando, Gerardo, Ramón, Antonio, and René as well.

In this battle to win our patriots' freedom— which will be like a rebirth, a resurrection for them when they return home—both peoples can support each other and fight together in solidarity until Oscar and Avelino are brought home to us and until Fernando, René, Gerardo, Ramón, and Antonio are brought back to their homes in Cuba.

APRIL 30, 2012

'ANGOLA MADE ME GROW'

By René González

In 1977–79 René González took part in an internationalist combat mission in Angola, one of the 375,000 Cuban volunteers who, between 1975 to 1991, helped defeat invasions of that newly independent African country by the apartheid regime in South Africa. The following interview was printed in the June 13, 2005, issue of the Cuban daily *Trabajadores*.

In the 2001 frame-up trial of the Cuban Five, González was convicted of charges of failure to register as a foreign agent and conspiracy to act as an unregistered foreign agent. In October 2011, after serving 13 years in prison, he was placed on "supervised release" and remains under court order to serve that additional penalty in the United States.

When González mentions the crime in Barbados he is referring to the 1976 bombing of a Cuban airliner that killed all 73 aboard moments after taking off from the Barbados airport. The bombing was organized by CIA-trained Cuban counterrevolutionaries Luis Posada Carriles and Orlando Bosch.

In April 1974 the dictatorship in Portugal was overthrown in the "Carnation Revolution," a coup by young military officers that opened the door to a mass popular upsurge.

Translation from Spanish is by the *Militant*.

René González Sehwerert's youthful spirit and internationalist sentiment came together in his life as a soldier during Angola's war of liberation. Trabajadores *reveals the feelings and motivations that brought one of our antiterrorist heroes to the African continent.*

I don't know if in the mid-1970s I would have needed too many reasons for carrying out an internationalist mission. It was in the air. Che's legacy was germinating. The empire's crimes wounded Cubans' collective sensibility with each news story of new aggression or of the latest military dictatorship making its debut or by directly wounding our own flesh with crimes like the one in Barbados.

Under those circumstances, the Carnation Revolution shook the Portuguese colonial empire like a breath of fresh air and opened up the doors to sovereignty for parts of Africa with which we were joined through centuries of exploitation.

When once again they turned to crime with the support and complicity of those who today try to give us lessons about human rights—apartheid South Africa had attacked the beginnings of a nation just starting to crawl in Angola—the Cuban people shook with anger. Trembling with anger myself and thanks to the help of some officials I managed to be included in the unit of my regiment that was assigned to carry out a mission. That's how I joined a tank battalion, as a gunner in an artillery crew, a day after having finished my three years of General Military Service.

Two years in Cabinda

After two months of training, the T-34 Tank Battalion arrived on the coast of Cabinda in March 1977. Our unit did not participate in combat activities; we were only a part of a defensive line shortly before returning, when the initial enthusiasm for the war on the part of the young troops had calmed down a bit, faced with the imminence of returning home.

Our initial amazement seeing the lush African landscape was followed by contact with an unknown culture and way of life. I was struck by the nobility, humility, and lack of malice of the Angolans, whom centuries of misery and exploitation had not managed to turn into predators. The word of any one of those peasants was worth more than the constitutions of all of the 'superior' countries that had gone to 'civilize' that continent.

An experience that had a big impact on me was seeing the hunger in the faces and bodies of the children. The look on their faces made you shiver. Through some tacit and silent agreement, each one of our two hundred combatants agreed, from the first day, to give up a portion of their meager rations to feed a dozen children who would wait for us by the side of the road three times a day as we were taking food to a small group of troops deployed near their village.

There are two juxtaposed moments that will forever be etched in my memory: those happy faces returning to their village and witnessing how a neighboring family was making a small coffin.

In the absence of combat, my stay in Angola coincided with the battle for the ninth grade. This task was taken on with enthusiasm; rustic classrooms were built in each company's area. I'm thankful to this assignment for my reconciliation with the lessons of mathematics, which I was able to teach. I had the satisfaction of seeing a group of officers and soldiers return to the homeland with a certificate showing the grade level they had conquered.

After two years of vigilance and intense prepa-

ration for combat, in March 1979 the last members of the T-34 Battalion of the Motorized Infantry Regiment of Cabinda boarded the ships that returned us to Cuba, with the satisfaction of having done our job and gone through a unique experience.

On the Zende hillock we left behind a renewed unit and a mountain of life experiences.

I never imagined that another experience—like the one I'm living now—would be able to go beyond the intensity and weight of the Angolan one in my upbringing and my life. That's the value that I see in my two years in Cabinda.

The work of imperfect men

That internationalist mission was the realization of a longing that made me grow as a human being. It wasn't all rose-colored. I had positive and negative experiences under difficult conditions. There I lived moments of tremendous joy and others of profound sadness; camaraderie was mixed with conflicts, I disagreed and I was in agreement, I got along with some and not with others, I made good friends or, simply, compañeros.

But each and every one of these experiences taught me something new and made me grow. I have gone back to that experience to resolve later problems, and each one of those combatants— perhaps like me at that moment without fully recognizing it—was a part of something much bigger than any one of us or even of our battalion.

The Angolan experience taught me that the most beautiful works are accomplished by imperfect men, each one of us a short impulse in history: that continual righting of wrongs that began with the first human injustice.

However, the role of Cuba in this epic poem was more than a short impulse. The push that the fight for Angola's sovereignty gave to the struggle against colonialism—that social cancer upon which opulence was built that today passes itself off as the civilized world—didn't stop until it reached the Cape of Good Hope, completely destroying the myth that was invented to enable them to carry out their policies of subjugation.

I think that it will be some time before humanity understands Cuba's altruism in Angola. In the individualistic world that is imposed on us, what someone has called 'sarcastic skepticism' corrodes

René González at age 21 in Angola, 1977, where more than 300,000 Cuban volunteers helped defeat US-backed South African apartheid regime's invasion there in the 1970s and '80s.

and immobilizes the collective consciousness forged in the masses, as a means of domination by those who build their fortunes on them.

But history is already written, at least up to this point, and the epic deed of our people in Africa is part of that. As it will be when all of the peoples united as one have sunk the bourgeois empire, erasing, at last, hunger from the face of the last child who has suffered from it.

DECEMBER 8, 2008

Support actions across Asia-Pacific

Above: Protest at US embassy in Colombo, Sri Lanka, July 26, 2011.

Below: Demonstration outside US embassy in Seoul, South Korea, September 12, 2008.

Above: After climbing Mount Ramelau, highest peak in East Timor, in support of Cuban Five, June 2012. Among the hikers were Timorese medical students trained in Cuba and Cuban doctors serving in East Timor.

Left: Perth, Australia, march for the release of the Five, September 12, 2011, on 13th anniversary of their arrest.

Among the Voices of Support

More than 350 committees in 114 countries, hundreds of political organizations, and thousands of individuals around the world are working to win the freedom of the Cuban Five. Below are a few of the prominent organizations, institutions, and individuals that have taken a stand against their imprisonment.

UNITED STATES

Legal organizations

Florida Association of Criminal Defense Lawyers
Howard University Law School, Civil Rights Clinic
National Association of Criminal Defense Lawyers
National Conference of Black Lawyers
National Jury Project
National Lawyers Guild

Trade unions and unionists

American Federation of State, County, and Municipal
    Employees Local 372 (New York)
American Federation of Teachers Local 2121 (San Francisco)
International Longshore and Warehouse Union Local 10
    (San Francisco)
San Francisco Labor Council
United Service Workers West–Service Employees
    International Union
Dolores Huerta, founding vice president,
    United Farm Workers of America

Religious organizations and officials

Interreligious Foundation for Community Organization
National Council of Churches
Thomas Gumbleton, former bishop, Detroit
Rev. Earl Kooperkamp, rector, St. Mary's Episcopal Church,
    New York

Government bodies and officials

City Council, Berkeley, California
City Council, Detroit, Michigan
City Council, Richmond, California
City Council, San Pablo, California
Ramsey Clark, former US attorney general
Cynthia McKinney, former US Congresswoman
Kurt Schmoke, dean, Howard University Law School;
    former mayor of Baltimore
Wayne Smith, former chief of US Interests Section, Havana
Esteban Torres, former US Congressman

Col. Lawrence Wilkerson (ret.), former chief of staff for US
    secretary of state Colin Powell

Organizations

Alianza Martiana (Miami)
Council on Hemispheric Affairs
Mexican American Political Association
National Latino Congress

Artists and writers

Edward Asner, actor
Harry Belafonte, actor
Mike Farrell, actor
Danny Glover, actor
Saul Landau, filmmaker
Graham Nash, musician
Bonnie Raitt, musician
Susan Sarandon, actor
Martin Sheen, actor
Oliver Stone, director
Gore Vidal, writer
Alice Walker, writer

FOR MORE INFORMATION:

www.thecuban5.org
International Committee
for the Freedom of the Cuban Five

www.freethefive.org
National Committee to Free the Cuban Five

www.granma.cu/miami5/ingles
Granma newspaper

www.antiterroristas.com

AROUND THE WORLD

Organizations

American Association of Jurists
Canadian Federation of Students
Ibero-American Federation of Ombudsmen
International Association of Democratic Lawyers
International Federation of Human Rights
Latin American Federation of Journalists
Mothers of the Plaza de Mayo in Argentina
National Association of Democratic Lawyers of South Africa
National Bar Association of Panama
Order of Attorneys of Brazil
Puerto Rico Bar Association
Student Federation of the University of Chile
World Federation of Democratic Youth

Trade unions and unionists

Association of State Workers (Argentina)
Bolivian Workers Federation
Canadian Union of Postal Workers
Canadian Union of Public Employees
Congress of South African Trade Unions
Inter-Union Workers Plenary–National Workers Confederation
    (Uruguay)
National Federation of Associations and Organizations of Public
    Employees (Panama)
National Federation of Teachers
    (Norway, Vesteralen region)
Oilfields Workers' Trade Union (Trinidad and Tobago)
Trades Union Congress (United Kingdom)
Unite (United Kingdom)
United Steelworkers (Canada)
United Food and Commercial Workers (Canada)
World Federation of Trade Unions
Ken Georgetti, president, Canadian Labour Congress

Parliaments

Argentina Chamber of Deputies
Bolivia Senate and Chamber of Deputies
Brazil Chamber of Deputies
Dominican Republic Senate and Chamber of Deputies
Mali National Assembly
Mexico Senate and Chamber of Deputies
Namibia National Assembly
Nicaragua National Assembly
Paraguay Chamber of Deputies
Peru Congress
Russia State Duma
Venezuela National Assembly
Latin American Parliament
Mercosur Parliament

Parliamentary groups and officials

Belgium, Flemish Parliament (35 members)
Canada Parliament (56 members)
Chile Senate (Human Rights Commission)
European Parliament (75 members)

Pickets in Vancouver, Canada, call for freedom of the Cuban Five, October 2007.

Germany Bundestag (65 members)
Inter-Parliamentary Union (50 members)
Ireland Parliament (55 members)
Italy Senate (39 members)
Panama National Assembly (president and vice-president)
South Africa National Assembly (president)
Switzerland Federal Assembly (48 members)
Turkey Grand National Assembly (Friendship with Cuba
    Parliamentary Group)
United Kingdom Parliament (112 members)
Miguel D'Escoto, former president, United Nations
    General Assembly

Religious groups and officials

Chamber of Anglican Bishops of Ecuador
Ecumenical Committee of Panama
Latin American Council of Churches
South African Council of Churches
Father Geoffrey Bottoms (United Kingdom)
Father Ernesto Cardenal (Nicaragua)
Khamba Lama Choijiljav Dambajav, vice president,
    World Fellowship of Buddhists

Nobel Prize laureates

Zhores Alferov (Russia)
Máiread Corrigan Maguire (Ireland)
Darío Fo (Italy)
Nadine Gordimer (South Africa)
Günter Grass (Germany)
Rigoberta Menchú (Guatemala)
Adolfo Pérez Esquivel (Argentina)
Harold Pinter (United Kingdom)
José Ramos-Horta (East Timor)
José Saramago (Portugal)
Wole Soyinka (Nigeria)
Archbishop Desmond Tutu (South Africa)

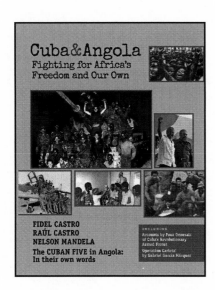

"Those not willing to fight for the freedom of others will never be able to fight for their own."

—Fidel Castro

JULY 1976

Cuba and Angola

Fighting for Africa's Freedom and Our Own

FIDEL CASTRO, RAÚL CASTRO, NELSON MANDELA
PLUS THE CUBAN FIVE IN ANGOLA—IN THEIR OWN WORDS

ALSO INCLUDES: ACCOUNTS BY FOUR GENERALS
OF CUBA'S REVOLUTIONARY ARMED FORCES AND
"OPERATION CARLOTA" BY GABRIEL GARCÍA MÁRQUEZ

From 1975 to 1991, some 375,000 Cuban volunteers fought alongside Angolan and Namibian combatants, defending newly independent Angola against multiple invasions by South Africa's apartheid regime.

Here leaders and participants tell the story of that milestone in the African freedom struggle and how it strengthened the Cuban Revolution as well.

Among those who explain how these experiences transformed them are three of the five Cuban revolutionaries today serving draconian US prison sentences on "conspiracy" and other frame-up charges.

$12. Also in Spanish.

www.pathfinderpress.com

From Pathfinder

MALCOLM X, BLACK LIBERATION, AND THE ROAD TO WORKERS POWER
Jack Barnes

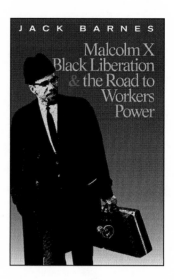

"Don't start with Blacks as an oppressed nationality. Start with the vanguard place of workers who are Black in broad proletarian-led struggles in the United States. The record is mind-boggling. It's the strength and resilience, not the oppression, that bowls you over."—Jack Barnes

Malcolm X emerged as the outstanding single leader of the US Black liberation struggle of the 1950s and 1960s. He insisted that colossal movement was part of a worldwide clash "between those who want freedom, justice, and equality and those who want to continue the systems of exploitation."

Drawing lessons from a century and a half of struggle, this book helps us understand why it is the revolutionary conquest of power by the working class that will make possible the final battle for Black freedom—and open the way to a world based not on exploitation, violence, and racism, but human solidarity. A socialist world. $20. Also in Spanish, French, and Arabic.

IS SOCIALIST REVOLUTION IN THE U.S. POSSIBLE?
A Necessary Debate
Mary-Alice Waters

In two talks—part of a wide-ranging debate at the Venezuela International Book Fairs in 2007 and 2008—Waters explains why a socialist revolution in the US is possible. Why revolutionary struggles by working people are inevitable, forced upon us by the crisis-driven assaults of the propertied classes. As solidarity grows among a fighting vanguard of working people, the outlines of coming class battles can be seen. $7. Also in Spanish, French, and Swedish.

TEAMSTER REBELLION
Farrell Dobbs

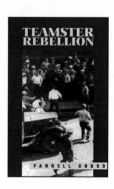

The 1934 strikes that built the industrial union movement in Minneapolis and helped pave the way for the CIO, recounted by a central leader of that battle. The first in a four-volume series on the class-struggle leadership of the strikes and organizing drives that transformed the Teamsters union in much of the Midwest into a fighting social movement and pointed the road toward independent labor political action. $19. Also in Spanish, French, and Swedish.

CUBA AND THE COMING AMERICAN REVOLUTION
Jack Barnes

The Cuban Revolution of 1959 had a worldwide political impact, including on working people and youth in the imperialist heartland. As the mass, proletarian-based struggle for Black rights was already advancing in the US, the social transformation fought for and won by the Cuban toilers set an example that socialist revolution is not only necessary—it can be made and defended. Second edition with a new foreword by Mary-Alice Waters. $10. Also in Spanish and French.

Books on the Cuban Five

United States vs. the Cuban Five: A Judicial Cover-Up
Rodolfo Dávalos Fernández
• **Editorial Capitán San Luis**
Cuban jurist Rodolfo Dávalos Fernández reviews every aspect of the US government's prosecution of the five men in the light of US and international law, legal tradition, and procedures. "From start to finish," he explains, "the proceedings were tainted, corrupt, null and void, vindictive. Every right of the accused to 'due process of law' was flouted." $22. Also in Spanish.

Hoping in Solitude
Antonio, Fernando, Ramón, René, Gerardo
• **Editorial Capitán San Luis**
A collection of poetry, essays, paintings, and music from prominent Cuban artists in honor of the Cuban Five. Edited by Cuban writer Eduardo Heras León, the volume includes statements of each of the five at their sentencing and at court hearings five years into their terms. $25. Also in Spanish.

Cuba, The Untold History
• **Editorial Capitán San Luis**
An account, fully illustrated and documented, of more than four decades of violent attacks against the Cuban Revolution by the US government—under ten different presidents. Defends and demands release of the Cuban Five. $32. Also in Spanish.

"The Dissidents"
Luis Báez, Rosa Miriam Elizalde
• **Editora Política**
In April 2003, seventy-five self-styled Cuban "dissidents" were tried, convicted, and sentenced to long prison terms in Cuba for acting as paid agents of Washington, organizing to undermine the revolutionary government of Cuba. This is the inside story. Who the "dissidents" were. How they were organized, financed, and directed. Based on testimony of Cuban revolutionaries who infiltrated their ranks and led some of the sham organizations. $24. Also in Spanish.

How Far We Slaves Have Come!
South Africa and Cuba in Today's World
Nelson Mandela, Fidel Castro
• **Pathfinder Press**
Speaking together in Cuba in 1991, Mandela and Castro discuss the place in the history of Africa of Cuba and Angola's victory over the invading US-backed South African army, and the resulting acceleration of the fight to bring down the racist apartheid system. Three of the Cuban Five served as volunteers in this internationalist mission. $10. Also in Spanish.

www.pathfinderpress.com

"One of the ways our revolution will be judged in years to come is by how well we have solved the problems facing women."

FIDEL CASTRO, 1974

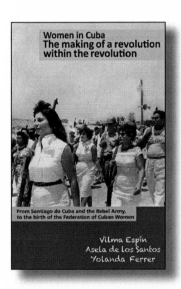

As working people in Cuba fought to bring down a bloody tyranny in the 1950s, the unprecedented integration of women in the ranks and leadership of the struggle was not an aberration. It was inseparably intertwined with the proletarian course of the leadership of the Cuban Revolution from the start.

Women in Cuba: The Making of a Revolution Within the Revolution is the story of that revolution and how it transformed the women and men who made it.

The book was introduced at the 2012 Havana International Book Fair by a panel of speakers from Cuba and the US.

Women and Revolution: The Living Example of the Cuban Revolution contains the presentations from that event. The example set by the men and women who made the Cuban Revolution, says Mary-Alice Waters, "is an indispensable armament in the tumultuous class battles whose initial skirmishes are already upon us."

Women in Cuba: The Making of a Revolution Within the Revolution

Vilma Espín
Asela de los Santos
Yolanda Ferrer
$20

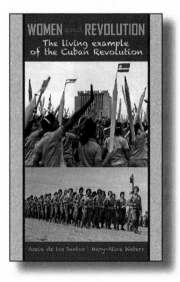

Women and Revolution: The Living Example of the Cuban Revolution

Asela de los Santos
Mary-Alice Waters
$7

Both titles also in Spanish.
WWW.PATHFINDERPRESS.COM

PATHFINDER

The Changing Face of U.S. Politics
Working-Class Politics and the Trade Unions

JACK BARNES

Building the kind of party working people need to prepare for coming class battles through which they will revolutionize themselves, their unions, and all society. A handbook for those seeking the road toward effective action to overturn the exploitative system of capitalism and join in reconstructing the world on new, socialist foundations. $24. Also in Spanish, French, and Swedish.

Lenin's Final Fight
Speeches and Writings, 1922–23

V.I. LENIN

INTRODUCTION BY JACK BARNES AND STEVE CLARK

In 1922 and 1923, V.I. Lenin, central leader of the world's first socialist revolution, waged what was to be his last political battle. At stake was whether that revolution, and the international movement it led, would remain on the proletarian course that had brought workers and peasants to power in October 1917. Indispensable to understanding how the privileged caste led by Stalin arose and the consequences for the class struggle in the 20th and 21st centuries. $20. Also in Spanish.

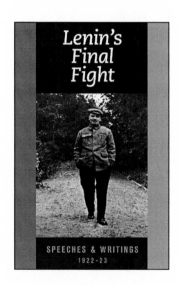

Cointelpro
The FBI's Secret War on Political Freedom

NELSON BLACKSTOCK

Describes the decades-long covert counterintelligence program—code-named Cointelpro—directed against socialists and activists in the Black and anti–Vietnam War movements. The operations revealed in the documents cited in this book—many of them photographically reproduced—provide an unprecedented look at the methods used by the FBI, CIA, military intelligence, and other US police agencies. Despite their authors' intentions, these documents also record pieces of the history of efforts to build the communist movement in the United States. $15

www.pathfinderpress.com

THE CUBAN REVOLUTION AND WORLD POLITICS

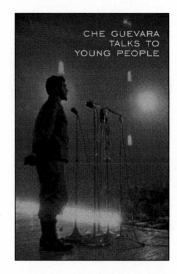
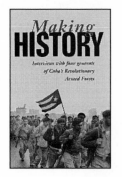

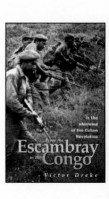

THE FIGHT FOR WOMEN'S EMANCIPATION

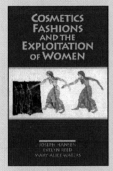

Cosmetics, Fashions, and the Exploitation of Women
Joseph Hansen, Evelyn Reed
Introduction by Mary-Alice Waters
How big business plays on women's second-class status and social insecurities to market cosmetics and rake in profits. The introduction by Waters explains how the entry of millions of women into the workforce during and after World War II irreversibly changed US society and laid the basis for a renewed rise of struggles for women's emancipation. $15

Problems of Women's Liberation
Evelyn Reed
Explores the social and economic roots of women's oppression from prehistoric society to modern capitalism and points the road forward to emancipation. $15

The Origin of the Family, Private Property, and the State
Frederick Engels
Introduction by Evelyn Reed
How the emergence of class-divided society gave rise to repressive state bodies and family structures that protect the property of the ruling layers and enable them to pass along wealth and privilege. Engels discusses the consequences for working people of these class institutions—from their original forms to their modern versions. $18

Women and the Cuban Revolution
SPEECHES AND DOCUMENTS BY FIDEL CASTRO, VILMA ESPÍN, AND OTHERS
Edited by Elizabeth Stone
The transformation of women's economic and social status in Cuba since the 1959 revolution. $16

New International
A MAGAZINE OF MARXIST POLITICS AND THEORY

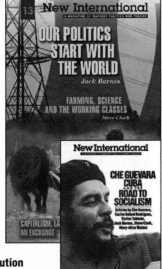

NO. 13
Our Politics Start with the World by Jack Barnes, Steve Clark • **Farming, Science, and the Working Classes** by Steve Clark • **Capitalism, Labor, and Nature: An Exchange** by Richard Levins, Steve Clark $14

NO 8
The Politics of Economics: Che Guevara and Marxist Continuity by Steve Clark and Jack Barnes • **Che's Contribution to the Cuban Economy** by Carlos Rafael Rodríguez • **On the Concept of Value** and **The Meaning of Socialist Planning** two articles by Ernesto Che Guevara $10

NO. 11
U.S. Imperialism Has Lost the Cold War by Jack Barnes • **The Communist Strategy of Party Building Today** by Mary-Alice Waters • **Socialism: A Viable Option** by José Ramón Balaguer • **Young Socialists Manifesto** • **Ours Is the Epoch of World Revolution** by Jack Barnes and Mary-Alice Waters $16

NO. 6
The Second Assassination of Maurice Bishop by Steve Clark • **Washington's 50-Year Domestic Contra Operation** by Larry Seigle • **Land, Labor, and the Canadian Socialist Revolution** by Michel Dugré • **Renewal or Death: Cuba's Rectification Process** two speeches by Fidel Castro $16

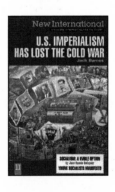

any of the articles that have appeared in **New International** are also available in Spanish in **Nueva Internacional**, in French in **Nouvelle Internationale** and in Swedish in **Ny International**.